James Chichester-Clark

Prime Minister of Northern Ireland

Clive Scoular

with a Foreword by

Paul Bew

Published in 2000 by
Clive Scoular
Killyleagh
County Down

ISBN 0-9539601-0-2 (paperback edition)

ISBN 0-9539601-1-0 (hardback edition)

Printed in Northern Ireland by
W & G Baird Limited
Caulside Drive
Antrim
Northern Ireland
BT41 2RS

For my parents,

Bill and Maureen,

with fond and enduring memories

Contents

Foreword

Clive Scoular's 'James Chichester-Clark – Prime Minister of Northern Ireland' fills an important gap in our understanding of the recent history of the 'Troubles'. James Chichester-Clark was, in many ways, a typical Unionist leader of the 'old school'. Born into a landed gentry family, he was educated at an English public school – in his case Eton – before seeing service in the Army and then returning to Northern Irish politics.

In following this pattern, he was very similar to three of the four Unionist Prime Ministers who preceded him – Sir James Craig (1921-1940), Sir Basil Brooke (1943-1963) and his own kinsman, Captain Terence O'Neill (1963-1969). This is a world with many profound associations which had a decisive impact on Northern Irish political life, but which has largely been forgotten about today.

Clive Scoular's memoir – lively, well informed and lightly written – recreates and evokes a highly significant connection which touched the lives of many people. He throws considerable light on the personal life of the Prime Minister but he also illuminates the dark side of the troubled period of the Province's history.

Paul Bew
Department of Politics
The Queen's University of Belfast
March 2000

Introduction

My interest in twentieth century Irish history has brought me into contact with not only the events in northern and southern Ireland at the beginning of the century, but also more recently with the men who became Prime Ministers in the north and Taoisigh in the south. Theirs are fascinating stories but, on examining what has been written about the northern premiers, I found a number of obvious gaps. Some titles have appeared over the years on Craig, Brookeborough, O'Neill and Faulkner, but nothing about the second and fifth Prime Ministers, John Andrews and James Chichester-Clark. I decided to try to remedy one of these omissions and determined to write a biography of James Chichester-Clark, whose premiership coincided with arguably the most difficult years of the Province's history, 1969-1971. Any passing references to Chichester-Clark in other books have been, at best, unhelpful and misleading and, at worst, positively damning and harmful, and so I considered that future Irish historians would not thank this generation for its negligence.

I have now attempted to remedy this oversight. I present, not a polemic of his political career alone, but a life story of this courageous and honourable man which, of course, includes the part he played in the years of his premiership. The biography of a man who, whilst perhaps destined to be a politician, never had any great desire to be Prime Minister does, nevertheless, acknowledge the faithful discharge of his duties in exceedingly trying circumstances. This giant of a man, though often shy and diffident, has, behind his granite face, a determination which few have ever appreciated.

I wish to put on record my thanks for the courtesy shown to me, at all times, by Lord Moyola and his wife as I spent many hours with the former Prime Minister at Moyola Park in the preparation of my work. I would also like to express my indebtedness to the members of the Chichester-Clark family and to many of their friends and former political allies for the help they have given me.

James Chichester-Clark was never solely a politician and Prime Minister. He was also a soldier, and a brave one at that. He is, too, a family man and one who has spent his life in the service of others.

It will now be for the reader to assess his place in Irish history.

Clive Scoular
Killyleagh
January 2000

1

The Purchase of the Cabbage Garden: The Dawson Ancestry

Today Moyola Park stands in spacious grounds of sweeping lawns and sumptuous gardens, surrounded by deciduous woods and ancient yew trees. It is bordered by the freely flowing and majestic river Moyola to the west and the narrow road leading off towards the Glenshane Pass to the east. There are over 450 acres in this fine arable estate with sheep and cattle quietly grazing its pastures. The peace is only disturbed by the click of golf club on ball as intrepid golfers take on the challenge of the picturesque 18-hole course, which lies on the south-western boundary of the estate. On Saturdays, when the local Moyola Park Football Club team* is playing a home match, there are a few raucous cheers which momentarily break the idyllic peace of the place. During the season, the burst of shotgun sunders the air, as the shoot gets under way in pursuit of pheasant and other hapless game fowl. This is the picture of the Moyola estate at the turn of the millennium.

It was not always so. In bygone years, from the early part of the 17th century, a big house has always stood there and squire, peasant and artisan have tended to the needs of the land and its people. Castledawson is its name today, but the village at the edge of the estate was formerly Dawson's Bridge, named after the family which, for centuries, has inhabited the estate house. The village is joined to the estate by a fine stone arch bridge over the river Moyola. It was built in 1710 and was the widest single span bridge in all Ireland at that time and for years to come.

---

* Moyola Park Football Club was the club which won the first ever Irish Football Association Cup in the 1880/81 season with a 1-0 win over Cliftonville. The match took place at Moyola Park.

Life was to change radically for the ordinary people of Ireland from the beginning of the 17th century. King James I decreed that land in Ulster should be 'planted' and given to Scots and English men of power and position. The more westerly counties were to be carefully fortified and those to whom land was given by the King had only a short time to build either castles or reinforced houses to defend their newly acquired lands from the marauding native population. So it was that the county, today known to some as Derry and to others as Londonderry but then known as County Coleraine, was given, in large measure, to the London Companies to 'plant', to own and to fortify. Thus came the salters and the clothmakers, the vintners and the drapers, the grocers and the merchant tailors to these relatively fertile lands of western Ulster. Lands were taken and houses and defences built pursuant upon the orders of their monarch. A chance such as this – of free lands and a ready workforce – was an opportunity not to be missed. And so towns like Draperstown, Bellaghy and Magherafelt sprung up and all over the county there appeared impressive mansions and castles with the new landlords safely there ensconced. The locals were hardly happy with this new arrangement, but they could do little about this new state of affairs.

However not quite all of this county remained in the hands of the London Companies. Two areas granted to Sir Thomas Phillips by King James I around Limavady and in the south east of the county were sold by him in 1622. The land to the south-east – 'the eight towns of Moyola', bounded by salters' and vintners' lands – consisted of almost 500 acres of good land, which Phillips had called the Cabbage Garden. His sons sold this land to Thomas Dawson and it was on this estate that he built the first Moyola Park House.

Thomas Dawson had not been quite the first Dawson to settle in Ireland for his father, Christopher, had arrived and settled in Ireland in 1611. Thomas, therefore, following the decree that fortified houses had to be speedily built on the sequestered lands, raised the first Moyola Park House in 1633. This mansion was not built on the site of the present day house but on a site close to where the church at the edge of the estate now stands. There still exist some remains of the original house for those who care to seek them out. For that house did not last long. At the end of the 17th century, it was unceremoniously pulled down to be replaced by a suitably impressive house on more open ground close to the attractive Moyola River. This house was completed in 1713, during the time of Joshua Dawson, a great grandson of the Thomas who built the first house.

The Dublin connection

To those who regularly visit Dublin, Dawson Street is a busy and important thoroughfare with good quality shops, formal office blocks and the attractive St Anne's Church. Close by is St Stephen's Green, Trinity College and the bustling Grafton Street. However the finest building on Dawson Street is undoubtedly the Mansion House. It is a building admired by all who see it. But most will not know of its pedigree. Not only is the Mansion House one of Dublin's oldest houses, but it was built by Joshua Dawson MP as his private house in 1710 on land bought by him in 1705. And so this famous street was owned by the Dawsons of Moyola Park in County Londonderry. Joshua, a beneficent and generous man, who was also Chief Secretary of State under Queen Anne in 1710, left this wonderful legacy to add to the many magnificent buildings in Dublin which, at that time, was considered as fine a city as there was in the whole of Europe. In 1715, after only five years living there, Dawson sold the house to Dublin Corporation and it has served as the Mansion House, the official residence of the Lord Mayor, ever since that date. The price to the Corporation for this worthy house was £3,500, a rent of 40/- and a loaf of double refined sugar weighing 6lbs at Christmas. Joshua Dawson also parted with many of his household effects including 6 marble chimneypieces, several tapestry hangings, various curtains and some gilt leather hangings. Although the house's original red brick appearance was altered in the 19th century, the Mansion House, which predates London's Mansion House by twenty years, remains basically the same splendid home of Joshua Dawson from Moyola Park.

A family of Members of Parliament: a family born to serve

Over the centuries, the Dawsons have served as Members of Parliament for Londonderry City and County in Westminster and, during the 20th century, in the Northern Ireland House of Commons. Joshua Dawson's son, Arthur, who was born in 1698, became firstly an MP and then a judge. He is of such importance that two paintings of him hang in Moyola Park. Both seem identical, but one is a copy and it takes an experienced connoisseur to tell the original from the copy. Nonetheless the family considers that both should continue to adorn the chief staircase and the dining room lest this baron of Chancery should ever be forgotten.

Arthur's nephew, also named Arthur, and who was born in 1745, inherited the estate on the death of his uncle. It was during Arthur's tenure of Moyola Park that the second house was accidentally burned down and he saw to the building of the third, and present, house in 1768. This house was built very close to the site of the second one, close to the Moyola River, but just a little further back from it. He, in turn, was succeeded by his son, George Robert, who is remembered perhaps as the greatest Dawson of them all.

George Robert Dawson was born in 1790. As soon as he entered young adulthood, he went into politics, which was nothing unusual for a Dawson. When Robert Peel was Chief Secretary in Ireland in 1812, George Robert became his secretary. In 1816 he met and married Peel's daughter, Mary. In the previous year, he had become the Member of Parliament for County Londonderry and he represented this constituency for the next 15 years until 1830. However, in August 1828, at a meeting of Apprentice Boys in Londonderry, he completely shocked his audience of fervent Orangeman and Apprentice Boys by declaring his full support for Catholic emancipation, saying that, regardless of his erstwhile views on the subject, he could now see no alternative to giving Catholics the vote. Needless to say, having seriously displeased his audience, he now had no option but to seek another seat. He was no longer welcome in Londonderry.

He did not have to wait long for the English seat of Harwich soon became available and he became their MP. He represented this constituency for just two years and then he returned to his Londonderry seat in 1832. In the harsh times which followed in Ireland, culminating in the Great Famine of 1847-1851, he remained mainly at Moyola Park where he freely dispensed food and nourishment to the starving people of the village and surrounding countryside. He was a caring and benevolent landlord, unlike many others who took the opportunity to simply put those who could not pay their rents (and these were practically all) off the land. In such regard was George Robert held that the people had a fine monument erected in his honour, after his death in 1856, in Christchurch parish church in Castledawson.*

George Robert Dawson's heir was his son Robert Peel who was born in 1818. Robert had only a single issue of his marriage, a daughter,

---

* This church was built as a private chapel for the Moyola Park estate and it was subsequently taken over by the Church of Ireland diocese of Derry in 1876, not many years after that Church's disestablishment in 1869.

Mary, and so it was that from 1856, on the death of Robert, there was no longer a Dawson as the squire of Moyola Park.

Chichesters, Clarks and Chichester-Clarks

Mary Dawson duly married and she took as her husband Lord Adolphus John Spencer Churchill Chichester, known as Spencer. This Chichester was a direct descendant of Sir Arthur Chichester* who had been James I's Deputy, or Lord Lieutenant, in Ireland at the time of the plantation of the western counties of Ulster.

The son of Spencer and Mary, Robert Peel Dawson Spencer, born in 1873, inherited the estate when his father died in 1901. He married, in 1902, Dehra Kerr-Fisher. They had just two children; a son, Robert, born in 1902, and a daughter, Marion Caroline Dehra, born in 1904. Young Robert was an ill and sickly boy who succumbed in 1920, aged just 17. Robert himself died in 1921 at the early age of 48 and so the Chichester line was abruptly ended.

Dehra Chichester was a formidable woman in her own right. She was gazetted OBE in 1918, which was advanced to DBE in 1949 and further to GBE in 1957. She took up politics and became MP for the County and City of Londonderry in the Northern Ireland Commons. She was returned, both in 1921 and 1925, by proportional representation (after 1929, this method of voting was changed by the Northern Ireland parliament to a 'first past the post' system). But in 1928, Dehra remarried and her second husband, Admiral Henry Parker, had his home at Leigh Court, Craddock in Devon. Consequently she virtually left Northern Ireland and had little or no time for attendance at the Northern Ireland House of Commons. Fortunately a solution presented itself. The next year, 1929, her son-in-law, James Clark, resigned from the Royal Navy which enabled her to resign her parliamentary seat. He then succeeded to the South Londonderry seat but was its member for just four short years until his early death in 1933. Dehra

---

* Sir Arthur Chichester (1563-1624) was Lord Deputy of Ireland under King James I in the early part of the 17th century. A hard working Deputy, Chichester completed the shiring of Ireland in 1616 and continued the policy of the ongoing plantation of the island. In 1608, he crushed a native rebellion in Inishowen and, as part of the King's policy of suppressing Catholicism, forbade Catholic children from being sent abroad to be educated. He shaped common law in Ireland and prosecuted bardic schools in order to curtail the native population's enthusiasm for a further restoration of the use of the Irish language.

was then pressed to return from England to regain her former seat and, not particularly liking Devon, she was only too pleased to return. She successfully regained the seat at a by-election in 1933 and then held it unopposed in the general elections of 1933, 1938, 1945, 1953 and 1958. She was only opposed once, and that was by the nationalist, T. B. Agnew, in 1949, when she won by over 3,000 votes. After being a Member of Parliament for 35 years, holding several government posts during this time, she retired, at the age of 78, in 1960. Her grandson, James, was to become that constituency's MP upon Dame Dehra's retirement. Dame Dehra died on 28 November 1963, her second husband having predeceased her in 1940.

In 1922, on her 18th birthday, Marion Chichester married James Clark who, having been born in 1884, was almost 20 years older than his teenage wife. He was also, in fact, just two years younger than his mother-in-law, Dehra Chichester. Clark had had a distinguished career in the Royal Navy, which he joined as a boy in 1899. He rose through the ranks from lieutenant, in 1906, until he reached the rank of captain in 1929. During World War I, he served with courage and bravery in the Red Sea and the Dardanelles. He was awarded the DSO in 1916 which was followed, the next year, by a bar to the DSO. He was also a Chevalier of the Legion of Honour, an Officer of the Crown of Belgium and was awarded the Croix de Guerre avec palme. He retired from the navy in 1929.

In 1924, James Clark decided to change his name by deed poll from Clark to Chichester-Clark. Although the Chichester name had died out, the fact that Clark had taken this name into his new double name meant that it would not entirely disappear. James Clark now had the unusual distinction of having two double-barrelled names. His full name became James Johnston Lenox-Conyngham Chichester-Clark. The Chichester-Clarks had three children – James, born in 1923, Robin, born in 1928 and Penelope, born in 1929.

When he retired in 1929 from the Navy, J. J. L-C. Chichester-Clark became the Member of Parliament in the Northern Ireland Commons – then still meeting at Assemblies College in Belfast – for South Londonderry. He spent time at Parliament in Belfast and much time at home with his wife and young children. Tragedy struck the family in 1933 when, on 31 January, whilst on holiday in Switzerland, Chichester-Clark died. His children were very young; James barely 10, Robin 5 and Penny only a little over 3 years of age. Mrs Chichester-Clark was only 29 years old and she now had her young family to bring up. By this time James was at school in Broadstairs in Kent and Robin and Penny were still at home. Robin had a

Swiss governess with whom he did not get on terribly well, When he was 8 years old he too went off to school in England to Selwyn House, Broadstairs where his brother, James, had been a pupil.

In 1938, Mrs Chichester-Clark remarried. Her second husband was Mr Charles Brackenbury. After the end of World War II, the Brackenburys went to live in the United States of America where they remained for five or six years. They then went to live in Geneva in Switzerland where Mr Brackenbury worked for the United Nations Organisation and there they spent most of their married life. They returned to Moyola Park each year for a month or so, but for the remainder of the year their County Londonderry property was cared for by staff. Mrs Brackenbury died in November 1976, aged 72. After cremation, her ashes were buried in the quiet and peaceful churchyard at Castledawson Parish Church surrounded by her illustrious forebears. Mr Brackenbury, now aged 90, continues to live in Switzerland and the Moyola Park family still keep in close contact with him.

During the final, troublesome years of the Northern Ireland Parliament at Stormont, much was made of the fact that James Chichester-Clark and Terence O'Neill, his predecessor as Prime Minister, were cousins. It was through the ancient historical branch of the O'Neills that they are remotely related. Therefore, when people describe these men as 'cousins', the relationship is hardly a close one. As it happens, Chichester-Clark is also a far out relation of Northern Ireland's third Prime Minister, Lord Brookeborough. Brookeborough's second son, John, who succeeded to the Viscountcy on the death of his father in 1973 and who himself died in 1987, was married to Rosemary Chichester of Galgorm Castle in County Antrim.

Thus were the O'Neills and the Chichesters interrelated and accordingly were yet more of Ireland's landed gentry thrust into public service to which they had become accustomed. Service to monarch and country has been the hallmark of this ancient Dawson line.

2

An Ulster Childhood: An English Education

James Chichester-Clark, born at home at Moyola Park on 12 February 1923 when his young mother was barely 19 years old, had a happy and interesting childhood. He appreciated something early on in his life – he really enjoyed being at home. He loved his familiar surroundings and the beauty of the local countryside. And so whenever he was at school in England as a young boy, or at Eton when he was a youth, he longed for Moyola Park.

At Moyola Park, then, James started his education, not at a local primary school, but at home with governesses. This was in no way unusual for children such as he. The sons and daughters of Ulster's 'big house' squires generally started their education at home, by way of preparation for public school in England. And the Chichester-Clarks were no exceptions. There were two governesses in James's early and formative years. The first, who arrived in Castledawson when James was six years old, was an unnamed Frenchwoman of whom little is remembered. The second, however, was a Miss McLean, a Scotswoman from the Perthshire town of Dunblane. James had a good relationship with Miss McLean and, under her tutelage, he learnt his three 'Rs'. She remained his governess until he was nine years old, at which time he left home to attend a private school in England.

Selwyn House School

Selwyn House School, one of many preparatory schools in the fashionable east Kent resort of Broadstairs in the 1930s, was housed in a fine Queen Anne house in spacious grounds. The running of the school, which never had more than 90 pupils, was a privately owned family concern. The first headmaster when it opened in 1906 was Mr Arthur Glyn Price until his sudden death in 1921. His widow and her second husband, Mr Robin Crawshaw, then ran the school until 1938. For the remainder of its existence, Mr John Green, son-in-law of Mr Price, was headmaster. The school closed in 1977 at a time when such small private schools were no longer in vogue. The house, however, remains standing and has been converted into apartments.

Here the young heir to Moyola Park spent four relatively happy years, from May 1932 until June 1936. At Selwyn House, Chichester-Clark remembered the headmaster as a tolerant and likeable man who seemed to enjoy the pleasures of golf as much as the welfare of his many young charges. James was particularly good at soccer and rugby, but his chief sporting interest was that most English of all games – cricket. Such was his proficiency and keenness in cricket that he was awarded school colours. He proved to be a middle-of-the-road pupil; steady, but not particularly outstanding. He did not win any scholarships, but he soon became a class monitor and eventually head boy. He did, however, make any number of school friends. He recalls one particular boy, Tony Langdon-Down, an English boy with whom he made a lasting friendship. Tony came visiting to Moyola Park on many occasions and it was during one of his stays that he and James incurred the wrath of the adults by severely damaging one of the river boats whilst dragging it across the Moyola river waterfall close to the house. But this was simply one way of learning to grow up. Sanctions were just and swift, but soon forgotten. And this friend, Tony, still keeps in touch after over 60 years. He still comes to Moyola Park from time to time when he is over in Northern Ireland visiting his relatives in the Ballymena area where his wife comes from. Like James, he too joined the forces during the war. He entered the Royal Air Force and saw much service during the conflagration.

Selwyn House was also to become the preparatory school for Robin Chichester-Clark from 1936 until 1940 and, during Robin's time there, the school was evacuated to Wales to avoid the London blitzes during World War II.

The journey to school in England in the nineteen thirties and forties was a complicated affair especially, at the outset, for a nine-year-old. James would be accompanied from Castledawson to Belfast to either the Liverpool or the Heysham overnight boat. There he would be put in charge of a friendly stewardess who would then ensure that, after a good night's sleep, he caught the morning train to London. At the station another family friend or acquaintance would meet the young Chichester-Clark, take him for lunch somewhere in the capital and finally ensure that he boarded the Broadstairs train at Victoria station. His journey from Castledawson to Broadstairs could, therefore, have taken all of twenty-four hours.

By the summer of 1936, it was time for James to leave Selwyn House. He sat and passed his common entrance examination for Eton and, after another enjoyable and idyllic vacation at home, he arrived at Eton the following September.

Interludes and vacations

Family holidays for the Chichester-Clarks were often spent in the little village of Culdaff in County Donegal. There James, his brother, Robin, and sister, Penny, would accompany their parents to stay two or three weeks in a cottage, close to other family members and friends. The young James would practise the art of shooting which his father had taught him. Many other equally enjoyable vacations were spent in Gstaad in Switzerland where James became a proficient skier. It was, sadly, during one of their winter vacations there that his father died of pneumonia when James was just 10 years old. After this James looked to other friendly adults to teach him other skills. On the little Donegal rivers, he was taught the gentle art of fishing by another man who, in his day and generation, was to serve his country. This gentleman was Mr Richard Pim who, in the days of the Second World War, was to work with Winston Churchill in his war office map room in London during the height of the conflict. In later years Sir Richard, as he was to become, became Inspector General of the Royal Ulster Constabulary (RUC) from 1945 until 1961. Holiday times at Culdaff and in Switzerland were wonderful breaks from the day to day routine at Moyola Park.

But Donegal and Switzerland were not the only locations for vacations for the Chichester-Clark clan. Their maternal grandmother, Dame Dehra Parker, lived for part of each year in lovely inland Devon and the children had many wonderful times there as well. James, when he was at Eton, would oftentimes travel direct by train to his grandmother's Devon home as soon as term was over. He thoroughly enjoyed his times there in the company of family and friends. Holidays were idyllic and were a time of fun and contemplation. They were ever to be remembered.

Eton College

Eton College is one of England's most prestigious public schools. Many would say, with conviction, that it is the best of England's public schools. It was founded in 1440 by King Henry VI, whose intention it was to ensure a fine education for the best in the land. The college became the centrepiece of the town of Eton and it continues to dominate the town to this day. There has always been a close relationship between town and gown and this also remains the case right up to the present day. It has been a school for the sons of the rich and famous and still continues to attract significant numbers of baronets and the sons of baronets, as well as a smattering of royal princes.

Eton is renowned for its traditionally classical standard of education. Each year dozens of old Etonians are accepted for the Oxbridge colleges. Upon graduation, many enter Holy Orders, others become lawyers, yet more become Members of Parliament and perhaps the highest percentage enter the army. There remain, too, its fair share of eccentricities with school titles such as Masters and Dames, praeposters and wet bobs, poena and Pop.

Into these hallowed portals in the autumn of 1936, James Chichester-Clark duly entered. In this school of 1,100 boys he was a good and steady, if not a brilliant, pupil. As a tall boy, he wore the high collar and full tailcoat, the uniform of that establishment. Had he been a shorter boy he would have worn, in place of the tailcoat, a short jacket. There he got down to study, enjoying most of all his history classes under Mr Routh, a Master whom he grew to like. James remembers many of the Masters: Marsden, Conybeare, Cattley, Lyttleton, Hamilton, Marten, Martineau and Gladstone, a direct descendant of the famous Prime Minister. Marsden, known to boys and Masters alike as 'Bloody Bill', was a disagreeable man, but the others, particularly Walter Hamilton, were decent and friendly.

As a boy belonging to Whitfields House, he got to know a number of the redoubtable Dames of Eton. Boys rarely saw their Dame unless one of them was ill. James recalls one of the most famous of the Dames, Miss Iredale-Smith, who was, in fact, his House Dame for a while. As boys grew older and more companionable, some of the Dames spent time with them and often sat down and talked to them. Otherwise they remained formidable and aloof.

Whilst he was a pupil at Eton, James well recalls the infamous 'fagging' and beating that went on. It was a way of life in the 30s and 40s and, as a 'lower' or junior boy, he had to 'fag' for senior boys. He was beaten once or twice, but not very often. Presumably as a tall boy in his junior years he was at some advantage over smaller boys. When he himself became a senior boy in his last year at school, he remembers his 'fags' and readily admits to beating one or two of them from time to time. But things have changed in recent times and he is happy that there is no more of this unnecessary barbarism at the school.

He was a popular boy and he participated, not in the world famous Eton Wall game*, but in the game known as the Eton Field game, a form of rugby, played only at Eton, with its own distinctive rules. The game was enjoyed, in inter-house matches, three or four times every week. But James' principal sporting activity was undoubtedly cricket. He played for his house as wicket keeper, a position which he thoroughly enjoyed for he was always able to see exactly what was going on in the match. Some loud – and sometimes rather dubious – appeals from behind the stumps often brought their rewards with the soulful batsman having to 'walk' earlier than he would have hoped. Occasionally he would also have joined in a game of tennis or even entered a boat to row on the river.

There were lots of other societies at Eton, such as the debating society, but James did not join in, preferring a book to read. Neither did he join the Scout Troop at the school. He declared himself as not being an enthusiast for these types of organised activities.

But, all the while, he longed to be back at home at Moyola Park. The first day of every term meant one day nearer the next school vacation. School holidays from both Broadstairs and Eton were, thankfully, long and idyllic. To a young man cooped up at school, any possible subterfuge was used to escape its clutches – even for a day – and the opportunities to do this increased as he became more and more senior at Eton. James tells the story of how he managed to feign a mysterious illness just to be able to go up to London to see a doctor. Not much is remembered about this particular incident apart from the satisfaction of having successfully hoodwinked the ever-watchful Eton authorities. This was a moment to be savoured.

When James was at Eton, the Headmaster was Dr (later Sir) Claude Elliott. He was, like all other Heads, a pillar of society who left his mark on the school during his 16 years there. He was a popular Head with the boys and James remembers breakfasting with him occasionally. It seemed that

---

* A rough and vigorous game played only at Eton.

Elliott was anxious to get to know his pupils and often invited perhaps half a dozen boys to come and join him for breakfast. James considered that this was a very agreeable method of building up relations between boys and their Head.

Whilst at Eton, early in 1940, the local Bishop came to the school and confirmed James and a number of his friends. He found the confirmation service most uplifting and was impressed by what His Lordship had to say. Sunday service was usually something that he found quite tolerable. Never being musical, however, he did not sing in the choir. During his sojourn at Eton, James met a number of other boys whose names were to become well known in future years. He knew the writer and broadcaster Ludovic Kennedy and John Floyd, chairman of Christie's from 1976 until 1988.

World War II impinged on the lives of Masters and pupils alike. The quinquennial celebrations due in 1940, for example, were postponed until after the war. The decision was taken not to evacuate the school. Air raid shelters were built, not entirely without opposition, and James remembers the one occasion when he had to use one of them. On the night of the terrible air raids on Coventry, the boys and Masters were told to use the shelters. They found them uncomfortable, but realised that they were a necessity of war. Masters and pupils became members of the local Home Guard to protect the school and its surroundings and James, already a member of the army corps, also joined. He recalls the school being damaged by incendiary devices which caused the destruction of the nearby music master's house. The boys often heard the loud explosions from raids in Windsor, only a mile or two distant. In a fire caused by enemy action towards the end of the war, and after James had left the school, two boys were killed when their house was burned down.

A number of friendships were formed at Eton and, when it came his time to enlist when war broke out in 1939, James soon realised that very many former Eton boys were joining up too. Most would become officers – a tradition of service in HM forces most common in all English public schools. Eton was no exception for it has produced countless famous soldiers, sailors and airmen, many of whom had offered the final sacrifice in so many world conflicts. Its record of service to King and country in the Second World War was outstanding. 5,000 young former Etonians enlisted and, of this large number, no fewer than 748 were killed, an extremely high percentage by any yardstick. Old Etonians won five Victoria Crosses, three George Crosses, three George Medals, 254 Distinguished Service Orders,

355 Military Crosses and 61 Distinguished Flying Crosses. Amongst this contingent of brave Old Etonians to join up, was the young squire of Moyola Park.

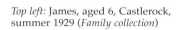

Top left: James, aged 6, Castlerock, summer 1929 (*Family collection*)

Top right: James, aged 8, Gstaad, Switzerland, winter 1931 (*Family collection*)

Centre: James, aged 11, on a hillside in County Antrim summer 1934 (*Family collection*)

Left: James, aged 11, at school sports at his preparatory school, Selwyn House, Broadstairs, Kent, summer 1934 (*Family collection*)

Right: James, aged 11, with his friend, Tony Langdon-Down, at Moyola Park, summer 1934 (*Family collection*)

Left: James, aged 8, skiing with his grandmother, Dame Dehra Parker, at Gstaad in Switzerland, winter 1931 (*Family collection*)

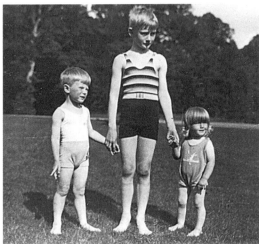

Right: James, aged 8, with his brother, Robin, aged 3, and sister, Penny, aged nearly 2, at Moyola Park, summer 1931 (*Family collection*)

Below: B.G. Whitfield's House at Eton College with James Chichester-Clark extreme right on second back row, summer 1937. The well-known writer and broadcaster, Ludovic Kennedy, is seated second from left. (*C. J. Parker c/o Eton College Photographic Archives*)

3

Called to Serve King and Country

When James left school in the summer of 1941, he contracted a throat infection which was to keep him 'hors de combat' for some months. This, of necessity, meant that his wish to join up as soon as possible was delayed. Then there was the family dilemma as to whether he would follow his father into the navy or his grandfather into the Irish Guards. His grandmother's influence won and, early in 1942, he joined the army at the barracks in Omagh, County Tyrone. It was not long before he found himself at training camp at Caterham in Surrey. There he spent three months in basic training in preparation for becoming an officer and, after nearly another year in various camps, the young Chichester-Clark was ready for the field and war action.

Ordered to take a train from St Pancras station in London, he knew he was being sent to join the war effort but unaware of any of the details. He did not even know his destination on boarding the train at St Pancras station. Its destination turned out to be Glasgow and there a troop ship awaited the recruits. The mystery of that ship's destination soon became evident. It was headed for the port of Skikda (formerly Philippeville) in Algeria.

By this time, July 1943, the North African campaign was over. After reversing the German forces at the famous battle of El Alamein, General Montgomery had led his victorious 8th Army westwards through Egypt and Libya and finally into Tunisia where he pushed Rommel and his Afrika Korps into the sea. This gruelling campaign, which had cost the Allies so many lives, had turned Allied fortunes at long last. The long awaited invasion of Europe was at hand. Sicily was retaken after two months of bitter fighting and mainland Europe finally beckoned.

At this stage, Chichester-Clark found himself joining up with the Irish Guards in northern Tunisia who were preparing to make their contribution to the war effort. They were soon on their way.

The Anzio landings

Rather than embarking for Sicily, Chichester-Clark's regiment headed by troop ship for the Italian West Coast. The main force landed at Naples on 22 January 1944. This was the commencement of Operation Shingle, the code name for the Anzio landings. This enormous taskforce left Naples on 21 January and began landing on the Anzio beachhead on 22 January. These forces, consisting of over 30,000 men and over 5,000 vehicles transported to the beach at Anzio by a huge convoy of 354 ships of all sizes and shapes, made an unopposed landing, much to everyone's surprise. Churchill and his generals had been satisfied that the assault at Anzio had gone so well but, when the story came to be written about this campaign, it is generally agreed that the forces should have pressed home their advantage as soon as they had secured their positions. They lingered too long, thus allowing the German commander, Kesselring, to muster his motley forces and to turn an almost certain defeat into what was to become almost an unlikely victory. In the end, however, despite heavy casualties on both sides, the Allies did manage to reach their goal – the Eternal city of Rome. The author, Martin Blumenson, in his book *Anzio: the Gamble that Failed*, sums up the fiasco at Anzio as follows: 'For the Allies, Anzio had become an epic stand on a lonely beachhead. But this description could not obscure the heartache. The outcome of the landing was one of the greatest disappointments of the war. The amphibious assault did not produce the result expected, the quick capture of Rome. By the merciless logic of war, the operation was a failure'.[1]

On 4 February, Chichester-Clark landed at Anzio, amidst the chaos around the beach, where he joined other regiments of the Irish Guards. The Battle for the Thumb was going badly and the Germans, under the aristocratic General Eberhard von Mackensen, were forcing a counterattack. It even looked as if the Allies might be thrown back into the sea. It was a fearful time to join the fray with the Irish Guards already suffering appalling casualties.

---

[1] Martin Blumenson, *Anzio: the Gamble that Failed* (London 1962) p. 188

Wound and recuperation

Into this ghastly theatre of war, therefore, Chichester-Clark and his men were thrown. It was to be, for them, a costly, bloody and short campaign. Not long after Chichester-Clark's company had set out from the Anzio beachhead, they were engaged in a life and death struggle for the little town of Carroceto on the road to the Alban Hills. Beside the malaria infested swamp land, the German forces were pushing them back. The Allied troops were virtually surrounded by enemy forces and the Irish Guards were on dangerous and exposed ground. For almost three weeks they barely managed to hold off enemy attacks, whilst continuing to suffer heavy losses. On 23 February, when seeking out some of his scattered men, Chichester-Clark was struck by an enemy projectile fired from many miles off. The shrapnel from this missile hit him in the back and on his left ankle. He had been seriously wounded and was terrified at the thought of being paralysed. He could not feel any sensations for some time after the blow and was relieved when feeling did return to his body. By that time, he had been taken to a nearby field dressing station where his injuries were tended to and where tiny pieces of shrapnel were removed from the wound in his back. There he remained for four or five days before being sent to a hospital in Naples for a further two weeks. His recuperation continued at Sorrento. His hospitalisation lasted, in total, for two months until the end of April. Writing about this critical period from 21-25 February the author, Carlo D'Este, graphically describes what was happening: 'During the three days and four nights the Irish Guards occupied the Boot they were under almost continuous attack. As bad as their earlier experiences had been, this one was even worse, a brutal, horrific existence that exceeded anything Dante might have conceived as a vision of hell. This was war at its absolute nadir, aptly described by the historian of the Irish Guards as "unremitting drudgery"'.[2]

The fact that Chichester-Clark had been wounded undoubtedly prevented further injury or almost certain death, for what remained of his company found themselves in the fiercest, bloodiest fighting, in a struggle to stem the German counterattack. Such were the heavy casualties in these days and weeks until the end of February that the Irish Guards ceased to exist as a fighting force. 'In barely more than a single month of combat the

---

[2] Carlo D'Este, *Fatal Decision – Anzio and the Battle for Rome* (London 1991) p. 288

1st Battalion, the Irish Guards, lost 32 officers and 746 enlisted men, 414 of whom were missing in action'.[3] All but 8 or 9 of Chichester-Clark's officer colleagues had fallen and died. He had known a number of these men very well and he was saddened at the news of their deaths. Now he experienced a kind of numbness which enabled him to overcome 'the sting of death'. His regiment had been so depleted that the few who were left, including Chichester-Clark, were shipped back home. Not long before they were transported back to Britain, they had a morale-boosting visit from Earl Alexander, who was himself an Irish Guardsman. His visit did much to raise the spirits of those who had survived. The journey home was not without incident. The Irish Guards embarked on the 'Capetown Castle', a large requisitioned liner, for their voyage to Liverpool. But returning to Britain was not a straightforward affair. The ship had to sail almost as far as the eastern seaboard of the United States before returning to the north-west of England. This was the route to be taken to avoid contact with the marauding German U-boats. They arrived safely at Liverpool but not before being exposed to a smallpox scare on board.

Chichester-Clark would not see any further war action. On arrival back home, he was sent to a barracks in the bleak, but beautiful, Scottish border town of Hawick. There he continued with his training for the best part of a year, where he also had frequent opportunities to pursue his much loved sports of fishing and shooting. He then moved down to the Guards' barracks at Caterham where he continued training young soldiers. As the war progressed he fully expected to be made ready for further service on some battleground, but this was not to be. He clearly remembers the day the war ended. He and some friends were on a week's leave in Sutherland in the north of Scotland. As they entered the little town of Lairg, they were greeted by a local woman who said, 'you'll be happy people, the war's over'. They were glad indeed.

James Chichester-Clark had, then, served his King and country in the Italian campaign and had been wounded as a result of his participation in the war effort. He realised how fortunate he had been. He had been one of the lucky few Irish Guards survivors who had lived to tell the tale.

---

[3] Carlo D'Este, *Fatal Decision – Anzio and the Battle for Rome* (London 1991) p. 290

4

Post War Career in Canada and England

And so the war had ended, with James Chichester-Clark having fought and been wounded in action. The remaining days of the war in 1945 brought a time of quiet and relief to him. He found himself posted, in late 1945, to Germany – now a conquered nation. The peace had to be upheld and so he spent more than a year in two locations in that battered and forlorn country. Firstly he was stationed in a small town close to Cologne and then he was sent to Hamburg. His job there, as he described it, was 'to keep the Germans in order'. They were a starving nation fed, in large measure, by the British forces. There were never any difficult incidents, but it was not an altogether pleasant task.

On a break back home in Northern Ireland in 1947, Chichester-Clark was spending his leave with a friend, fishing in County Fermanagh. In the midst of this, one of his very favourite pastimes, came a visit from a policeman from the local barracks. Chichester-Clark was asked to make a call to his regimental Headquarters in England. As he made his way to the nearest telephone, he wondered what the message would be. Captain Chichester-Clark was asked if he would like to go to Government House in Ottawa, Canada, to become an ADC to the Governor General, Earl Alexander of Tunis. Lord Alexander was, of course, an Ulsterman, the third son of the Earl of Caledon, and Chichester-Clark accepted the posting without hesitation. Not only was Lord Alexander a fellow countryman, but he was also another Irish Guardsman, like Captain Chichester-Clark.

It was not long before Chichester-Clark was aboard the 'Empress of Canada' sailing for Montreal in Quebec. Before embarking, he had done some preparation by reading about his new boss. Earl Alexander of Tunis and of Errigal had been a wartime hero, chosen by Winston Churchill over the head of yet another Ulsterman, Alan Brooke, to become the last non

Canadian to be Governor General of that vast country. He had greatly looked forward to this new challenge and, at the age of 55 in April 1946, together with his young wife and three young children, set off to undertake his duties as the King's representative. The King, George VI, and the Canadian Prime Minister, W. L. MacKenzie King, had unhesitatingly chosen Alexander over other prospective candidates. In his six years in Ottawa, Alexander endeared himself to the Canadian people. Not only did he regularly meet with them, but he also freely and enthusiastically participated in their sports of bowling, skiing and ice-skating. He was a popular man and one who, whilst being formal when the occasion required it, could easily blend in with the local population.

Thus prepared, Chichester-Clark went directly to Government House to meet the Governor General. Rideau Hall, the Governor General's official residence, was a huge semi-Paladian mansion in parkland close to the Ottawa River. In a part of this great house was quartered the secretariat, headed by Major General H. F. G. Letson who had a fairly large staff which included 'two British ADCs (of whom one for a period was James Chichester-Clark, later Prime Minister of Northern Ireland)'.[1] These days, from 1947 until 1949, were happy and pleasant times. Whilst Chichester-Clark had great admiration for his boss, who was 'an extraordinary and wonderful man', even so, he did not fully warm to him. Alexander was meticulous about punctuality and detail and yet he gave much responsibility to his ADCs, including Chichester-Clark. There were a great many visits to be organised and, during his two years there, he travelled with Alexander all over the country by train and by aeroplane. Chichester-Clark remembers being two or three times as far west as the beautiful Province of British Columbia. This was the most spectacular part of Canada after the monotonous flatlands of Saskatchewan and Manitoba. He always considered that the last 500 miles were the ones most worth seeing.

He found Canada a lovely and fascinating country and felt fortunate that he had been given the opportunity to spend time there. He enjoyed many fishing trips with the Governor General and others of the staff and there exists much photographic evidence of his success in catching many a fine fish taken from those wild and wonderful Canadian rivers. He liked the people and met, on more than one occasion, the Prime Minister, MacKenzie King, whom he described as approachable and

---

[1] Earl Alexander, *The Alexander Memoirs* (London 1962) p. 291

pleasant. He did not return to the British Isles during his two year spell in Canada and, although he had loved the experience, he was pleased eventually to return to his beloved Moyola Park for some leave before moving on to his next posting.

Last years in the army

Upon his return from Canada early in 1950, Chichester-Clark rejoined his battalion in Germany. There he stayed, as part of the occupying power, for a further three years until 1953. Life in Germany was never very exciting but he was able to see an improvement in the lot of the impoverished German nation. By 1953, he had a new posting to the Middle East. He moved to Egypt, a country which he never liked. He and his battalion took on the role of administering an area outside Cairo as part of the British forces who were in Egypt as a quasi occupying force. He left this 'his least favourite and most boring place' in 1954. He was soon back again in London before going to the Staff College at Camberley. Here he spent a year improving his skills as an officer but, by now well into the late 1950s, he felt he had spent sufficient time in HM forces. It was time for a change in his life and this was certainly to come sooner rather than later. His final posting was back home as a Deputy Assistant Quartermaster General, Northern Ireland Command, and a new life and direction were panning out before his eyes.

5

Family:
This Generation of Chichester-Clarks

Family is important to us all. It is every bit as important to a politician. It is essential to a Northern Irish politician. James Chichester-Clark owes much to his family. For centuries his forebears have offered themselves as Members of Parliament, both at Westminster and in the Northern Ireland House of Commons. In recent times, both his father and his maternal grandmother have served the people of South Londonderry. And from 1960 until its prorogation in 1972, James continued the family tradition by fighting for the causes close to the hearts of the people of that constituency in the Northern Ireland House of Commons at Stormont. As Prime Minister from 1969 until 1971, he brought added responsibilities and pressures to his family.

In consequence they deserve mention, if only to remind us that politicians are not a race apart, but have the links of the common man – with wives and children, brothers and sisters. Here I present vignettes of his wife, Moyra; his daughters, Fiona and Tara; his stepson, Michael and his brother and sister, Robin and Penny.

Moyra, Lady Moyola

Moyra Maud Morris was born in Buncrana, County Donegal, the only child of Brigadier Arthur and Mrs Doreen de Burgh Morris. Her father had come from an old ascendancy family from County Galway and her mother was the daughter of Sir Henry Miller of Carrigans, County Donegal, a one time Mayor and town clerk of Londonderry. Doreen Miller was to become the Irish ladies' golf champion in her youth.

As the Brigadier was a Gurkha officer, the Morris family spent most of their lives in the Indian sub continent. It was in this lovely climate that the young Moyra enjoyed her early days and some of her early schooling. In Assam, in Pakistan, and in the valleys of the beautiful Himalayas, she came to love the outdoor life, where she learnt to ride horses in her exploration of the breathtaking mountain passes. Here, too, she mixed freely with the Indian people whose children were to become some of her closest childhood companions. However, she was soon to leave this idyllic surrounding to go to England where she commenced her formal schooling. As she grew older she came to County Armagh to continue her education, before eventually ending up in the Dublin School of Art. She looks back on her varied education with much pleasure, but admits to have relished her two years of school in India as those which made the greatest impression on her. From those early days in the East emanated her lifelong love affair with travelling, and there remains scarcely a part of the entire world which Moyra has not visited.

When back in Northern Ireland she met and married, in 1950, Captain Thomas Haughton, the only son of Major Samuel Haughton who had been Westminster MP for South Antrim from 1945 until 1950. Tommy Haughton had joined the Royal Inniskilling Fusiliers in 1940 before being commissioned in the Royal Irish Rifles the next year. During the 'D' day landings, he acted as ADC to Sir Richard Gale, one of the Allies senior commanders, and it was for his services at this time that he was mentioned in despatches. He survived the war to return home to join his father's bleaching and finishing business of Fraser and Haughton in Cullybackey, County Antrim. Sadly, however, he was not to survive long in peacetime.

Disaster at Nutt's Corner

On Monday evening, 5 January 1953, an Admiral class airliner (a converted Viking) took off several minutes late from Northolt Airport, near London, bound for Belfast. There were 31 passengers, including one baby, and four crew on board. This was a scheduled flight in those relatively early days of commuter air travel to and from London and Northern Ireland. Apart from some persistent cloud around Belfast, the night was clear. As families and friends awaited their relatives at Nutt's Corner, they saw the outline of the aeroplane approach. But their joy at the expected arrival of their friends changed very quickly into horror. As they watched, the aircraft struck a telegraph pole and a runway building and burst into flames, crashing into a field at the edge of the runway. Several small fires immediately broke out and, as fire crews and some of those waiting dashed across the runway, it was obvious that death and destruction was to meet them. It was clear that the aeroplane had been destroyed and that there would be many casualties and fatalities.

As grim reality sunk into the minds of panicking friends and relatives, a tragedy of immense proportion was upon them. Of the crew of four, three were dead and of the 31 passengers, 24 had succumbed. There were just eight survivors. All were taken to the nearest hospital, the Massarene in Antrim. Compared to the scene of utter devastation at Nutt's Corner, peace and calm pervaded the wards and corridors of the hospital as nursing and medical staff fought feverishly to preserve the lives of those passengers who had survived. Many had been very seriously injured and, as they struggled for life, little did they know the fate of their fellow travellers on this ill-starred flight. This had been the first civil air accident which British European Airways had suffered at Belfast.

Amongst the terribly injured was Moyra Haughton, by then expecting her first child. As she lay in the hospital suffering from a broken neck, she was soon to learn that her young husband, who had fought so courageously in the Second World War, had died in the crash. She was now a widow after less than three years of marriage. Sadly, she was not able to be present at the funeral of her husband, which took place on Wednesday, 7 January at Craigs Parish Church in Cullybackey where Tommy had been a lifelong communicant and, of recent days, a member of the choir. He was laid to rest in the adjoining churchyard.

Life goes on

Although her injuries were serious, Moyra Haughton, her unborn child un-harmed, eventually recovered. Her life had to go on. She went to live at the Green Cottage in Cullybackey, a delightful little house belonging to the Fraser and Haughton company. There she made a home for her young son, Michael, who was born in June just after the Coronation, and there she remained until 1959.

By now she had met James Chichester-Clark and, after a whirlwind romance, the couple married on 14 March that year in St Columba's, Walton Street in London. Theirs was a quiet wedding with only a few close family friends as guests and, after their honeymoon, the couple returned to make their home at Moyola Park. The house had not been lived in permanently for some time and consequently the squire and his lady had to spend much time restoring the lovely house to its former glory.

When Chichester-Clark was returned to the Northern Ireland Parliament in 1960, the new Mrs Chichester-Clark, now the mother of a daughter, Fiona, began to become familiar with being the wife of a country squire who was also a Member of Parliament. Living 'above the shop', so to speak, meant that they were often inundated with constituents looking for fairness and justice from their MP and Mrs Chichester-Clark soon learned that this would be their way of life for some time to come. As the years progressed and her husband's parliamentary duties increased, so came the interminable outings to ploughing matches, to unionist meetings and to Women's Institute gatherings. Soon came the impromptu speeches and the constant grasping and shaking of sticky hands. Never far away were the planting of trees and the presentation of cups to farmers, to Scouts and to innumerable other worthies. In her estimation, women were considerably better at making arrangements than were men which meant that speeches were properly prepared for a women's meeting. A few quickly thought up words were all too regularly the order of the day for the men folk. The record number of speeches – both impromptu and prepared – which she recalls, was after a ploughing match in rural County Londonderry. 29 of the assembled company got to their feet to make a verbal contribution. Such were the vicissitudes to be faced by an MP's wife. When her husband was Minister of Agriculture and later, when Prime Minister, Mrs Chichester-Clark found herself present at many unpleasant and hectic gatherings, mainly in halls where noisy verbal tirades often turned into ugly physical fracas.

During the Prime Ministerial years, she was even busier than ever. From time to time she had to stay with her husband in a flat in Stormont Castle where she discovered the woeful and almost non-existent catering. Often the Prime Minister's wife had to return to Castledawson to prepare the food for visiting dignitaries who were at Stormont and then dash to Belfast to sit down at the dining table knowing that she and her friends and staff had made all the preparations. But she revelled in this activity and found being a Prime Minister's wife much to her liking – at least on these occasions. At Moyola Park she and her husband entertained visiting politicians, the most notable of whom were James Callaghan, Cledwyn Hughes and Reginald Maudling.

When James Chichester-Clark resigned in March 1971, Moyra Chichester-Clark was not dismayed. She knew that she and her husband would now have another chance to try to regain their former family life, although life at Stormont went on until 1972. But, later in 1971, her husband was ennobled as Baron Moyola of Castledawson and she became Lady Moyola. The title did not go to their heads for they continued to be involved in the farm and in the building of the golf course on their estate. This was hard physical work but a good antidote to years of political wrangling. The Moyolas now had time to enjoy their far off holidays, which continue to the present day. The last nearly thirty years have passed by watching their family grow up and by the arrival of grandchildren. Life is no longer so full of turmoil and disruption. Life is more tranquil, as befits the lord and lady of Moyola Park.

Robin

Robin was born at home at Moyola Park on 10 January 1928, the second child of his parents. He enjoyed home and all the opportunities the estate offered a growing and inquisitive boy; whether it was learning to fish in the Moyola river or building a tree house somewhere in the woods. He liked the company of his brother, James, who was five years older than him, but Robin was closer to his sister, Penny, who was just 22 months younger. As children they spent holidays in Switzerland, where they learned to ski, and also enjoyed many breaks in Donegal and in Devon.

Robin's father died suddenly of pneumonia whilst on holiday in Switzerland in January 1933, aged only 49. Robin quite vividly recalls the day of his father's funeral. Both he and his sister were very young and, as was the tradition of the time, children were not seen at funerals. He remembers his governess minding him in the upstairs nursery and relaying to him, through the curtains, what was happening outside. He regrets, even at this distance in time, that he had not been able to witness those sad events more closely.

To all young lads, holidays were much more fun than schooling and education, and so it was for Robin Chichester-Clark. In the early days he had governesses who taught him the rudiments of reading and writing but then, in 1936, aged 8, Robin moved to preparatory school at Selwyn House in Broadstairs, where James had also been a pupil. In 1939, shortly after the outbreak of World War II, the teachers and pupils of Selwyn

House were evacuated to a lovely house in Montgomeryshire in Wales. Robin loved being in Wales, out in the familiar countryside again. Here the 48 or so boys got very close to their teachers. There was a real sense of adventure and comradeship in being sent away from Kent, which was in direct line of any possible invasion by the Germans at that time. Robin loved this period of his life.

But he did not take to his next school – he positively hated it. For some obscure reason, it was deigned that Robin should become a sailor. Perhaps, because his brother was in the army following his grandmother's wishes, it was considered politic that Robin should pursue his father's naval career. But he never wanted to go to sea and, as a consequence, considered his time at the Royal Naval College to have been nothing short of a disaster. He was not in any way interested in navigation and things nautical but, as providence would have it, he was able to throw off these unwanted shackles before the end of his allotted time at Dartmouth. He contracted a duodenal ulcer which took him away from the college for some months. When he returned he was well behind in his work and promptly failed some examinations. Thus he was able to get out of the navy rather than having to be bought out. The illness had been a blessing in disguise.

Aged just 17 in the autumn of 1945, Robin, having sat and passed his entrance examinations, went up to Cambridge to study history and law. He now spent three years 'learning about life' but pursuing precious little study. However he successfully completed his degree and, as an adventurous young man, headed off to New York in 1949. He had gone to the United States to visit his mother and his stepfather, Charles Brackenbury, who worked at the United Nations there. Robin got himself a job with *Time* magazine to earn money with a view to travelling in that vast country. Having spent some time hitch-hiking and riding Greyhound buses, he soon returned to England. Simultaneously, he worked as a journalist with the *Portsmouth Evening News* and the *Hampshire Telegraph*. Then he became the Public Relations Officer with the Glyndebourne Opera and finally with the Oxford University Press which was to have been a career move to enter publishing full time.

But it seemed improbable that a Chichester-Clark should become a journalist. After all, the family had always produced politicians, not journalists. And so Robin did become a politician. In 1955, the Westminster seat of Londonderry City and County fell vacant. The sitting member was retiring, and Robin Chichester-Clark's name was put forward for the vacancy. The idea appealed to Robin and, after fighting off other prospective Ulster Unionist hopeful nominees, he was selected to fight the seat at the 1955 General Election. He was just 27 years old and, in the election, he easily defeated the Sinn Fein candidate, M. Canning, by over 16,000 votes.

Without a great deal of trouble, therefore, he was a Member of Parliament at Westminster, not quite the youngest, much to his disappointment, but the second youngest, the other being just two weeks younger. For the succeeding nearly twenty years, the name of Robin Chichester-Clark headed the poll at successive elections from 1955 until 1970. He was an ambitious member who soon stepped on to the rungs of the promotion ladder. In 1958 he became Private Parliamentary Secretary to the Financial Secretary to the Treasury, Jack (now Lord) Simon, before soon becoming an assistant Whip under Edward Heath, who was then Chief Whip. Further promotions within the Whip's office soon followed until he was one of the three most senior Whips, one of whose duties was to be in attendance on the Queen and Prince Philip. When the Tories went out of office in 1964, he became the chief Opposition spokesman on Northern Ireland, in which capacity he led debates and answered questions with more and more regularity. In addition, he also held the Shadow portfolios of the Arts and Public Buildings and Works. However, when James became Prime Minister of Northern Ireland in 1969, Robin, of necessity and at Heath's suggestion, took more of a back seat.

In 1972, with Heath now Prime Minister and his brother, James, now no longer Prime Minister of Northern Ireland, Robin re-entered the government as Minister of State at the Department of Employment. He remained in this post until the Conservative Government was defeated in February 1974. Robin decided not to stand again for his Londonderry seat. By now he had lost the stomach for politics. The trauma of the years when James was Ulster premier had made Robin realise that there was no longer a place for a broad minded and liberal man like himself in an Ulster Unionist Party which now possessed too many militants. He knew also that there were many who wanted to 'get at him' because of his brother. Rather than having an unholy row over the nomination – for which Robin knew he would never be selected – he got out, leaving the seat to the unimaginative and uninspiring William Ross, who has held the seat, nonetheless, ever since. There was his ignominious prosecution by the Orange Order following his attendance at the funeral of a Catholic friend of his. The service had, of course, taken place in a Catholic church and, as it was against the rules of the Orange Order to enter a Catholic church for any reason, their officials reprimanded Robin for what was, after all, clearly a personal and private matter. Soon afterwards, he resigned his membership of the Order.

During all his years as member for Londonderry, Robin had returned to Northern Ireland every weekend to visit the various parts of his constituency and to make speeches and open garden fetes, these being the staple diet of most politicians. As the time went by, he realised that being an MP and travelling backwards and forwards to and from London and his home at Kells, was putting an undue strain on his marriage. His first marriage ended in divorce in 1972. Yet it could never have been said that Robin Chichester-Clark was anything but a conscientious Member of Parliament. In the end he was not entirely sad to be finished with politics, for as he said himself, his heart was no longer in it. His departure from the political arena, at the early age of 46, was a real and genuine loss of 'an articulate and dedicated full-time politician'.[1] He has two daughters and one son by his first marriage and two sons by his second. All still live in the London area and all, including his two grandchildren, regularly visit him.

Links with his Prime Minister brother

Pleased as he was to see his brother enter Northern Ireland politics in 1960, never did he think that James had any great ambition and he certainly never thought that James wanted to accede to the top job as Prime Minister. Robin had always been a close confidant of Terence O'Neill's and had been most supportive of his reform programme. Indeed, O'Neill had often sounded Robin about his plans and was, at all times, anxious to hear from Robin what the MPs at Westminster were thinking of his reform packages. Robin agrees that O'Neill was uncomfortable with the common people but that he was genuine in trying to pull Northern Ireland into the twentieth century, to cast aside the lethargy and disinterest shown by his predecessor, Lord Brookeborough. Robin is convinced that O'Neill was not gesturing in his reforms but truly wished a better future for all the Province's citizens. But, in the end, O'Neill lost his way and, by early 1969, the writing was on the wall. James had, often with Robin's support and encouragement, made suggestions to O'Neill for further reforms. After the

---

[1] Ken Bloomfield, *Stormont in Crisis – a Memoir* (Belfast 1994) p. 73

disastrous events in Londonderry in October 1968, the Chichester-Clark brothers had counselled O'Neill that he must speed up his reforms and had even given him some helpful proposals. O'Neill seemed to reject these overtures and, as the months went by, James realised that there was no further worthwhile mileage in O'Neill. Robin is convinced that his brother resigned as Minister of Agriculture, not because of the 'one man, one vote' issue (which was simply a front and an excuse) but because he had lost confidence in O'Neill's ability to get things together and get more reforms carried out. O'Neill's persona would never let him get near to his people and it was time to 'wipe the sheet clean'. Thus Robin understood the reasons for his brother's resignation and told O'Neill exactly why James had resigned. O'Neill did not like what he heard from his good friend Robin Chichester-Clark and consequently had little more to say to him over the rest of his life.

Even at this juncture, James Chichester-Clark did not really want to be Prime Minister. But it was obvious to all that he would be a leadership candidate and he realised, with the encouragement of Robin and others that, although still reluctant to take on the job, he felt it was his duty to let his name go forward. He did not think that the alternative candidate was the right man for the job. In the end he became Prime Minister with the smallest possible majority and many commentators, both far and near, gave him very little chance of succeeding in the post. He was seen as a 'stop-gap'; one who could not last. Robin did not agree with these purveyors of doom and gloom. James had many strengths. He was absolutely straight, was without guile and had no axe to grind. He had extraordinarily good instincts for what the people would put up with and what he felt they really wanted. Admittedly his brother was not a born television performer and this put James Chichester-Clark down in the eyes of the critical public. With so many broadcasts to make during his premiership, he rather failed in this endeavour.

During the time when his brother was Prime Minister, Robin regularly kept in touch with the British MPs. He often gave advice to Harold Wilson and Jim Callaghan and later to Edward Heath and Reginald Maudling. He had, in fact, been giving counsel to senior politicians at Westminster as far back as the days of Sir Alec Douglas-Home. He became possibly the most vital link between Stormont and Westminster. He found Wilson tolerably good to get on with. He rather decried the rumours of Wilson's early days in power in 1964 when, with just a wafer thin majority of 4, he was reputed to have wanted Ulster Unionist MPs – then taking the

Tory whip – to have been barred from voting in the House. They were consistently voting with the Tories and continually making life difficult for Labour with such a slim majority. This, Robin declared, had been backbench pressure on Wilson and not a demand of his own. He was also a close friend of the enigmatic Edward Heath who, on occasion, had been Robin's guest at his home in Kells.

At the time of the Bogside riots in August 1969, Robin had been in his constituency and experiencing many of the difficulties common to those who represented the government's thinking. He knew that troops would have to be sent in and he continued to liaise between Callaghan and his brother at Stormont. This week in Londonderry had been for him the most traumatic of his entire time representing his constituents in that ancient, yet troubled city.

For the entire time that James was Prime Minister, Robin kept close contact with his brother and very often discussed tactics with him. He appreciated that James had only a very restricted pool of MPs from which to choose a Cabinet and from which to select other minor government Ministers. Too many of the unionist MPs were only at Stormont as 'time servers' and it would have been unthinkable to choose any of them for posts of responsibility. Robin realised that James was continuing to have many almost unbearable pressures upon him – from Paisley and Devlin on the one hand to recalcitrant unionist backbenchers and troublesome Ulster Unionist Council meetings on the other. When James resigned in March 1971, Robin knew the real reason for his brother's decision. It had always been put about that James Chichester-Clark resigned his post because he did not get the number of extra troops which he felt were necessary. Although there is an element of truth in this, the matter of 'no-go' areas was the major reason. Early on in Heath's premiership, after June 1970, Chichester-Clark had warned him that if 'no-go' areas were allowed to persist, then the local population in those parts would become used to the rebellious men who were taking charge and recruitment for the IRA would escalate. Heath did not listen to the Northern Ireland premier and Chichester-Clark's fears became the reality. 'No-go' areas became the breeding grounds for terrorists and the Queen's writ no longer held sway in those streets. Heath did not believe that James Chichester-Clark would resign but, on 20 March 1971, he did. An opportunity to continue the extensive reform programme had been lost, and lost for ever – not because of an Ulster Prime Minister who did not know where he was going – but because of the intransigence and obduracy of a British Prime Minister.

After giving up politics in 1974 and entering upon a second marriage, Robin undertook a number of interesting and worthwhile jobs. His chief interest has been working in various charity fields, particularly in those relating to literature and medical research and he remains involved and committed to these challenges. He now looks forward to a degree of semi-retirement in order to enjoy his home in London and his house in Somerset. His two youngest sons remain at home and Robin and his wife take as many opportunities to visit Moyola Park as possible. The draw of the wide-open spaces of Moyola Park still holds great sway with Robin Chichester-Clark for it was there that the chance to pursue the family interest in politics took hold all those years ago.

Fiona

Fiona Chichester-Clark, James Chichester-Clark's elder daughter, was born on 28 April 1960. She had her 9th birthday at exactly the same time as her father became Prime Minister of Northern Ireland. She was not best pleased, therefore, when all attention on that day in 1969 was focussed on her father and not on her. Birthday girls should, she thought, get all the limelight on their birthday. But instead of full attention from doting parents that day, it was banks of photographers taking pictures of her now famous father. However Fiona did garner some of the benefits of that auspicious day. A band from the village of Castledawson came up to Moyola Park where they played as a way of congratulating their local son on his elevation to the post of first citizen of Northern Ireland. And Fiona could then say that some wonderful music had been played at her house on the occasion of her 9th birthday. No one needed to know that the band was playing for her father's benefit.

But from then on, at least for some considerable time, things changed at Moyola Park. Squads of members of the RUC appeared as if by magic to take care of the Major, for Prime Ministers needed protection, especially in Northern Ireland in the late 1960s. Fiona and her sister, Tara, soon got to know these policemen and whenever they went off to some special occasion with their parents, the bodyguards came along too. They did not have their own bodyguards, simply because their lives were kept as private as possible. Fiona attended the primary school at Rainey Endowed School in Magherafelt until the summer of 1969. She then went off to school at Knighton House in Dorset, a girls' preparatory school with around 90 pupils.

Fiona was now away from all the limelight at home. Some of her school friends did enquire what it was like to be the daughter of a Prime Minister, but most did not even realise that their friend Fiona was any different from any other of their friends.

Fiona returned to Moyola Park for Christmas. She now saw a little more of her father, although he was often called away to some political event, and she learnt to deal with the fact that her father was needed elsewhere. However that Christmas holiday, her parents were able to take time off and go skiing in Switzerland. This was a very special holiday. Not only were they skiing for the first time and staying with their grandmother and step grandfather in Geneva, but they were enjoying their new sporting experience in the pretty Swiss town of Zweisimmen. And, while they were there, the local town councillors held a wonderful banquet in honour of their father. Fiona recalls this evening well. There she was, aged 9, sitting at a beautifully laid high table surrounded by the finest settings and glasses and eating the loveliest food. She listened while the admiring hosts wined and dined the Prime Minister of Northern Ireland and speeches were made by both host and visitor. Gifts were bestowed on their honoured guests and the little Chichester-Clark girls were not forgotten when it came to the receiving of presents. Fiona remembers the lovely sweater she received from their Swiss hosts. It had been an evening not to be forgotten. The next morning, on the ski slopes, there was a photo call when the girls and their parents were photographed by numerous paparazzi. They did feel like royalty – and for the day they were.

Back at Moyola Park, Fiona, her sister and her stepbrother, Michael, enjoyed the holiday break before they all returned to England to school. They continued to see little of their father and even their mother was required to be away from home quite a bit of the time. At home they were looked after by nannies, so there was never any difficulty in their being cared for when their parents were off meeting all manner of politicians. Fiona never met James Callaghan or Harold Wilson. She did, however, meet Captain O'Neill in the days before her father was Prime Minister. She has only a vague recollection of him, although she remembers how sweet Mrs O'Neill was. Fiona was rarely paraded before politicians and this was certainly never a source of regret to her.

She can remember being at a premiere of the film 'Battle of Britain' in Belfast and she thinks that the Queen might have been there, although she does not recall meeting the Sovereign. Fiona has a story of being at home one holiday at this time when she wondered at her little sister practising her curtsies. When she asked her why she was doing this, Tara replied that the Governor was due to visit and she must approach the Queen's representative in the proper manner.

The two years of her father's premiership went quickly by. Fiona did not see so much of him, although both parents occasionally visited her at preparatory school. She remembers once that her father was summoned back to Belfast as a matter of urgency during one of these school visits. Her stepbrother, Michael, had been at Harrow School for some time, but he spent holidays at Moyola Park too. The girls got on well with him, even though he was seven years older than Fiona and nine years more than Tara.

Life as a daughter of a Prime Minister had its advantages and disadvantages. But it did not last long. The Major resigned in March 1971 and life was largely back, if not to normal, at least to what it had been when he had been serving in the O'Neill Cabinet.

Before and after these two years, life had been enjoyable. The family often spent their summer holidays at Carrigans in County Donegal. Fiona's mother had come from that part of the world and there the de Burgh Morris family lived. Fiona liked being with her maternal grandparents and loved going fishing and messing about in boats with their parents. Donegal had, in years gone by, held an attraction for the young James Chichester-Clark too and the whole family seemed to learn to fish, shoot and sail boats in that far and delightful north-western Ulster county.

Fiona often asked her father about his earlier life experiences and stories from his youth. He was rather reticent, although he did often talk of his wonderful and fulfilling days in Canada with Earl Alexander. There he seemed to enjoy the best fishing of his life.

When Fiona left Knighton House she went to the girls' Public school, Cranbourne Chase in Wiltshire. There she stayed until 1976. By her own admission, she did not do so well at school and after spending that summer at Moyola Park helping to build the new golf course, she went to Bournemouth to try her hand at tennis. Although she did have considerable potential, this career did not work out and, with her mother's encouragement and support, she went to London to become an apprentice furniture restorer. This she enjoyed and she came home to Castledawson in 1979 to set up her business in the basement at Moyola Park. She remained in this profession until 1993, although she did move away from Moyola Park in 1988 to set up in Portadown. But, after all these years, with trade being difficult, she moved into other ventures until the present day when she and her husband now specialise in a shop in Portadown. Fiona married in 1994 and inherited three stepsons, the oldest of whom is in his early twenties.

Fiona keeps in touch with home and occasionally sees some of her cousins who live in such diverse places as London and the Scottish island of Oronsay. From time to time she would be in contact with her Uncle Robin (Sir Robin Chichester-Clark) in London and her Aunt Penny (Mrs Malins) who lives in Dorset in the south of England.

Tara

The Head Teacher came running into the classroom, full of excitement. 'He's been elected, he's been elected!' she exclaimed. The class teacher was obviously delighted too. The excitement rubbed off on the class of 6 and 7 year olds. 'Isn't that wonderful?', they thought, turning to the pupil next to them. Then they looked about and tried to figure out what all the excitement was about. Then it dawned on one six-and-a-half year old in the room that reference was being made to her father. Tara Chichester-Clark's father had just been elected Prime Minister of Northern Ireland. When asked by her friends that day 'was it not terrific that her father was now the Prime Minister'? Tara turned to them and replied, 'Well, he's just my Daddy and that's his job'. There could be no adequate response to such an innocent remark.

These events took place on 1 May 1969 in the Primary Two class at Rainey Endowed School in Magherafelt, County Londonderry. The teachers were excited because their esteemed Member of Parliament had just been elected Prime Minister and that sort of thing did not happen every day. On returning home from school, Tara found lots of things happening. There were photographers and journalists amassed outside the front door at Moyola Park. Tara and her sister were brought out to be photographed with their parents. The cameras clicked repeatedly and the flashguns startled the girls. They were certainly in the limelight. Things settled down next day, but Tara knew that, although it was only her father's job, nonetheless, life at Moyola Park was going to change for a time.

Tara had been born, at home, on 8 July 1962, the second daughter of her parents. Her sister, Fiona, was then a little over two years old. After her early education at Rainey Endowed School, she went to the girls' school, Knighton House in Blandford Forum, Dorset, in the autumn of 1970, when she was eight. There she joined her sister and about 90 other girls in this typical preparatory school in that lovely part of England. Later she went on to the girls' public school, Sherbourne House at Sherbourne in that same county of Dorset until she was 18 years old.

During the two years when her father was Prime Minister, life remained relatively unchanged at home. She did not see so much of her father and her nanny had to look after her often when her parents had to go off to various formal events. At Moyola Park there was now a caravan in the grounds, which was a police post. Tara got to know the friendly policemen who soon knew how to spoil their Prime Minister's young daughter. Politicians did come and go but Tara has little recollection of meeting any of them, although it does seem likely that she and her sister were trotted in to greet visiting dignitaries only to be ushered out again at speed. Holidays, even during these hectic years for her father, were still seen as important and they were enjoyed. Like her sister, Tara remembers the famous visit to Switzerland when the family was wined and dined by the Burgermeisters of the Swiss town of Zweisimmen. It was an enjoyable enough evening except for the interminable speeches and translations. But the food and presents made up for the boring formalities of the evening.

Recalling these years, Tara does realise that something different had happened at the time of her father's election. She knows that she certainly did not see him as much, but something did strike her at the time. Her father was often at Parliament Buildings at Stormont in Belfast until the early hours, rushing home for a couple of hours sleep before having to get back to Belfast as quickly as possible. But Tara remembers that he always made time to look into the farmyard to see how the animals were faring. This, she thought, was his way of keeping sane during all those days of ever increasing crises. And her mother, all the while, took everything in her stride. 'That's the kind of mother I have – moving quickly and efficiently from one situation to another'.

When Tara left school, she attended the university at Aix-la-Chappelle in France for an academic year, before returning to Magherafelt to undertake a secretarial course at the local Technical College. She went to London where she modelled for a time before becoming a secretary and eventually ending up as a conference organiser for the Asia Pacific region.

She met her husband, Edward Whitley, who came from a big brewing family in Cheshire, while she was in London and they married in 1984. They lived in Hong Kong from 1984 until 1989 when they returned to London before finally finding their ideal home in the picturesque village of Wilmington in East Sussex. They have a young son, James.

Being the daughter of a Prime Minister, at the time, seemed unimportant to Tara. Life at home was pretty normal and that just happened to be her father's job in life. Looking back, she realises what a strain it had been on him but, at the time, Tara was just mystified by all the media hype.

Penny

Penelope Chichester-Clark was born on 20 November 1929 and was, therefore, born nearly seven years after James and a little less than two years after Robin. Consequently, Robin and Penny were very much closer to one another, simply because James was so much older and was often away at school when they were small children enjoying fun at home.

In her early years Penny was educated at home, sharing a governess with some of her young cousins. Life and learning were thereby cosy without the strain of having to share the attention of a teacher with lots of other demanding youngsters. She quite well remembers Miss McLean, the Scottish governess of her older brother, James, but this slightly formidable lady never taught Penny. At the tender age of twelve, Penny left the comfortable surroundings of Moyola Park to be educated at school in England. She went, again with some of her cousins, to a girls' public school near Broadstairs in Kent. The school was at North Foreland, the most easterly place in all of Kent. But, having started there in the early years of World War II and with ever increasing air attacks by the Luftwaffe on London, Penny and her school mates were quickly evacuated to a lovely house in Gloucestershire and she never returned to North Foreland. School was enjoyable but, nevertheless, she did like the long school vacation when she could return home to Moyola Park.

Their summer holidays were often spent in Donegal and Robin was her constant companion. By now, James had joined the army and they only met each other rather infrequently. 'War was a funny time for we never quite knew where any of our family members were going to be'. But Penny did take a keen interest in her handsome older brother who, by now, was fighting in Europe. She was therefore stunned to hear, in a letter to school from her mother, that James had been injured in Italy in the battle of Anzio. She was subsequently very relieved to know that he was recovering and would soon be well again. During the war she only saw occasional glimpses of James but her mother kept her up to date with all his news.

After leaving school, aged 17, Penny went to Girton College at Cambridge University where she studied Economics and was successful in achieving a BA (Hons). At Cambridge she met Paul Hobhouse and, in 1952, they married. Three children were born of this marriage, a daughter and two sons. Nowadays Penny's older son lives in London and her daughter and younger son live in Scotland.

But Penny's life changed dramatically after her children grew up and left home. She chanced upon gardening as a career. She had always been interested in the garden, but now an opportunity came for her to take up this fascinating hobby seriously. For fourteen years, until 1993, she was the National Trust tenant of Tintinhull House in Somerset and here she had a wonderful opportunity to restore its gardens to their former glory. From 1976 onwards, Penelope Hobhouse became widely known as a garden writer and consultant. She took up writing and has written well over a dozen titles ranging from *The Country Gardener* in 1976, through *Private Gardens of England* in 1986 and *The Gardens of Europe* in 1990 to her present work on the world history of gardening. Penny is described in the fly leaves of her titles as 'a consultant with considerable experience of making gardens grow'. There is not a library in the land which does not stock titles written by Penelope Hobhouse. It can be said, with certainty, that hers has become the household name in gardening as Mrs Beeton's has always been in cooking.

In 1960, when her brother James took up his career in politics, Penny was not at all surprised. This was the family tradition and it was almost expected that James would follow where other Dawsons, Chichesters and Chichester-Clarks had gone before. He knew about politics and would be good at it. She had always been accustomed to political discussions in their home and she, like her brothers, had been exposed to the fiery prognostications of their formidable grandmother, Dame Dehra Parker. Whenever she got the chance, Penny spoke and discussed matters of political import with James. She was keen to follow his advancing career and also that of Robin, who had entered parliament at Westminster in 1955 which was even earlier than James's entry to Stormont in 1960.

However, when James was elected to the post of Prime Minster in 1969, Penny had mixed emotions. She knew he liked what he was doing and felt that he would do well in the post. When she saw the difficulties under which he was suffering, she knew that this would bode ill for a man who was basically hard working and modest and not a man fitted for the ungentlemanly behaviour to which he was daily exposed. She was relieved when he resigned in 1971. In these years, Penny met many of the local politicians and knew Terence O'Neill and his wife, Jean, very well. Lady O'Neill still lives in active old age relatively close to Penny in the south of England. She, too, is keen on gardening which makes their friendship even more meaningful.

In 1983, following her divorce from Paul Hobhouse two years previously, Penny married Professor John Malins, who had been a professor of medicine. They had met in gardening circles and Penny was greatly saddened when he died in 1992.

Penny keeps in close contact with James at Moyola Park and sees him as often as she can. Although she and her brother were not close as children, because of the obvious age gap, they have closely followed each other's careers as the years have passed by. It continues to be a great pleasure when the various members of the family have the opportunity to meet up again to discuss the contributions they continue to make to society.

Michael

When Michael Haughton was born, he was already fatherless. His parents had been involved in the horrific aeroplane crash in January 1953 which sadly claimed the life of his father, Captain Thomas Haughton. His mother, at that time four months pregnant, had miraculously survived and Michael was born in June 1953. Michael's early days were spent at the Green Cottage in the pretty County Antrim village of Cullybackey and there he was surrounded, not only by the loving care of his young mother, but also by the members of the Haughton clan who had lived in that part for many years. He had a happy childhood there where his constant friends were cousins and the neighbours' children. The absence of his father was compensated, to some degree, by his adoring maternal family.

In 1959, his mother married James Chichester-Clark and Michael's life radically changed. He now moved to live in the grand setting of

Moyola Park and, from his earliest days there, his stepfather became a wonderful companion and father to him. He was taught to shoot and fish by the Major and a firm bond quickly developed between man and boy. When Fiona and Tara were born, Michael became the loving older brother and childhood memories are of all three children happily enjoying their chief pursuit of riding, of spending time minding the farm animals and helping with the household chores.

He left home in the early 1960s to go to preparatory school at Ludgrove School at Wokingham, Berkshire, before eventually moving to Harrow School – that most prodigious of English public schools. Life was tolerable at school but holidays were always keenly anticipated. It was during his teenage years that James Chichester-Clark became Prime Minister of Northern Ireland. This elevation for his stepfather meant little to Michael at school in England and the fact that he had a different surname ensured that there were few or no enquiries as to what it was like to have a Prime Minister for a father. But when he came home on holiday during those years, he did have the opportunity to meet Terence O'Neill, Chichester-Clark's predecessor, although he has no recollection of meeting any of the English politicians who frequented Moyola Park from time to time. Summer holidays at Moyola were always thoroughly enjoyed and for his stepfather, in Michael's estimation, Moyola was home and Stormont was the office – straightforward reality for a perceptive teenager.

When he left school, aged 19, Michael travelled in Europe and the United States before settling into employment. His home has always been in London and there he married his wife, Tessa, in 1981. They continue to live there with their two children, Tommy and Cara, and they take as many opportunities as they can to return to Moyola Park for holidays.

6

A Move to Politics and Entry to Stormont

By the early part of 1960, the die had been cast. James Chichester-Clark, having considered a full time career in farming or in politics, had now made up his mind. He would enter politics to follow the family tradition, knowing that he would also have to farm the estate at Moyola Park. His grandmother, Dame Dehra Parker, now aged 78 and having been a prominent Member of the Northern Ireland for so many years, was very unwell and was being discreetly encouraged to resign her seat. Her decision, therefore, to resign was hastened by the fact that her grandson had determined on his new career and, since it was the inheritance of the Chichester-Clarks and their forebears to enter parliament and give service to their country, she did not find this a difficult step to take. Indeed, she was extremely pleased that James had shown a desire to follow in her footsteps. She felt she now wanted a rest for she had given sufficient of her life to politics. In fact, it was the second time in her life that she had stood down for one of her male relatives. In 1929, when she had already been serving the new Northern Ireland government for two terms, she had resigned her seat in favour of her son-in-law, James J. L-C. Chichester-Clark, who had just retired from the Royal Navy after a distinguished war career. Unfortunately, Captain Chichester-Clark died in the early part of 1933, thus leaving the South Londonderry seat again vacant. And so, once more, Dame Dehra stepped in and was restored to her erstwhile parliamentary seat. For 27 more years she served, both as a backbencher and then as a member of the Cabinet. She had been undoubtedly the most influential female member of the Northern Ireland parliament in the entire fifty years of its existence.

James Chichester-Clark, now 37 years old and recently married, took his first tentative political steps in June 1960. He sought the nomination for the now vacant South Londonderry seat and hoped for success in his endeavour. He soon discovered that his was not the only nomination. There was a second nominee in the race to fill the vacancy. This other candidate was another well-known and very active local Magherafelt Ulster Unionist, Mr R. A. Brown, who was also a leading light in the Farmers' Union. A meeting took place in Maghera on 6 July, when both candidates presented themselves to the local South Londonderry constituency members. In a close run fight, Chichester-Clark came out on top, by the slender margin of 110 votes to 93. The contest had been a clean one and immediately upon being selected, Chichester-Clark was congratulated by Mr Brown who promised the victor his full co-operation. Both men, in fact, became good friends and worked hard for the constituency over the years. The *Mid Ulster Mail* informed its readers that their new candidate, Major Chichester-Clark, had 'seen service in North Africa, Germany and the Middle East'.[1] They seemed pleased at the selection of yet one more of the Moyola Park dynasty to represent South Londonderry in parliament.

It was not long before Chichester-Clark was returned, unopposed, for South Londonderry. He was declared elected at Londonderry Courthouse on Saturday 9 July and then, as if he had endured a hard fought struggle to win the seat, he moved a vote of thanks to the returning officer and paid tribute to all the unionist workers in the constituency. This may have appeared an empty gesture, but it was one required by the traditions of parliamentary protocol. He was now a Member of Parliament – yet another in the long line of Moyola Park squires to hold the post. He was, in fact, now the dynasty's ninth Member of Parliament in just 100 years. The sleepy little towns of Bellaghy, Kilrea, Magherafelt and Maghera had a Member of Parliament once more.

July was, of course, not the best time for a new Member of Parliament to be elected. Parliament was in recess and would not be recalled until the end of October. Chichester-Clark was impatient to get to Stormont but he had to bide his time. He made good use of his new found freedom by coming to grips with the vagaries of farming, which now became his day to day occupation. This he came to love, although the differences from army life could hardly have been greater.

On 25 October 1960, Major James Dawson Chichester-Clark, the member for South Londonderry, was sworn in in the Stormont House of Commons. As he looked around, he could see the benignly smiling face of

---

[1] *Mid Ulster Mail*, 9 July 1960

the Prime Minister, Viscount Brookeborough, and a veritable sea of unionist members quietly wishing him well. Across the floor of the House on the Opposition benches, a smattering of Labour and nationalist members simply noted, with an air of indifference, the arrival of yet another unopposed unionist member. They wondered whether or not he could be as formidable as his predecessor, Dame Dehra.

'Could the Minister of Commerce state how many grant-aided industries have been set up in the parliamentary constituency of South Derry since the war'?[2] These were the first words uttered by James Chichester-Clark at Stormont. The date was 16 November 1960. The reply from the Minister, Lord Glentoran, was not very satisfactory to the ears of the young Chichester-Clark. Only one such industry had been given government support in that time, an answer which did not much please the member for South Londonderry. He instantly demanded a new advance factory for his beleaguered constituents and a shamefaced Minister scuttled off to harry his civil servants into action.

At that time, Stormont sat on just three days each week. Chichester-Clark made it his endeavour to attend on at least two of these days and, as often as possible, on all three days. As a backbencher and a 'new boy in the House', he did as much as he could to cultivate associations and friendships with as many members as possible. By now Brookeborough was in his last years as Prime Minister and he generally only came to Stormont one day per week. However, he was always keen to meet new members and Chichester-Clark found him quite approachable. He was 'always willing to chat to anybody'. Brookeborough had often chided Lord Craigavon for hanging on to office too long (Craigavon had been Prime Minister for over nineteen years). Yet he himself was Prime Minister for even longer and did not resign his office until he was nearly 75 years old. He remained a Member of Parliament until his 82nd year and most right thinking people considered this to be an entirely unsatisfactory state of affairs. It could be said that he hung, like an albatross, around the neck of his successor, Terence O'Neill. Perhaps it should have been that, once ennobled, Craigavon and Brookeborough ought to have had to resign from the Northern Ireland Commons. But so it was that peers of the realm were permitted to retain their Commons seats, unlike their counterparts at Westminster.

---

[2] *Hansard,* 16 November 1960

Before his first term was over, Chichester-Clark had asked the relevant Ministers about an additional number of matters. He enquired what advantages had accrued to the farming community from the lowering of the level of Lough Neagh; he insisted on the dredging of local rivers; he wanted to know more about the measures being taken by the Minister of Agriculture to prevent diseases in the potato crop. And, on 6 December, he asked a question about a matter which was causing his constituents some considerable problems. 'When was the new road bridge over the Bann at Toome to be completed'?[3] The answer did not impress Chichester-Clark and it was to take some considerable time to construct the necessary and vital road improvement which was greatly needed to assist his constituents in commuting to and from the South Londonderry area.

A worthy maiden speech

Major Chichester-Clark was, by now, becoming accustomed to parliamentary procedures in the House. He had attended regularly and had asked many incisive questions. He had made Ministers squirm from time to time. But he still had one important hurdle yet to jump. There was the matter of his maiden speech. By February, in his second term in the House, he now felt sufficiently confident. In the early afternoon of 8 February, he stood up, to thunderous cheers from his own supporters and, in a wide-ranging and lengthy speech, he pronounced with great conviction on the many and varying needs of his constituents. He reminded the House that unemployment in South Londonderry was 10%. This was unacceptable and government needed to pay more than scant attention to the problems of those living west of the Bann. His constituents had long journeys to make every day to get to their places of employment in Belfast, Ballymena or elsewhere and they had far too little time to spend with their families as a consequence of such long working days. More factories were urgently required in his constituency to attract more employment for the well-being of the people of South Londonderry. The speech lasted over half an hour and was listened to with interest by those assembled in the House. Chichester-Clark had made his mark.

In the remaining days of the term, until the summer of 1961, he spoke on yet more pressing matters. He showed his concern about the long

---

[3] *Hansard,* 6 December 1960

delays in bringing electricity to parts of South Londonderry. He compared the benefits of living in the cities and large towns to the difficulties of living in the countryside. He spoke on education and the need to improve the pay of teachers. From time to time, he alluded to his army service in his speeches in the House. There was the matter of the pasteurisation of milk – something which he supported – and he recalled the fact that, when in Germany after the war, it had been impossible for the starving German population, and for members of the armed forces of the Occupying Powers, to obtain any fresh milk at all. Milk was, therefore, an absolutely essential and vital commodity.

In the terms which followed in 1961, 1962 and 1963, Chichester-Clark continued to contribute to the ongoing debates in the House. His frequent interventions were primarily concerned with improving the lot of his own constituents. He demanded better transport, an improvement in financial support to farmers who had, through ill health, been deprived of their livelihoods and better care for school children who were stressed by taking examinations. On 28 March 1962, he had occasion to thank the Minister of Commerce for providing funds to expand a factory in South Londonderry. His pressure had obviously paid off – but he did not forget to remind the Minister of the need for further work. The Minister would not be allowed to lie back on his laurels.

James Chichester-Clark was, by now, attracting the attention of the Prime Minister and other Ministers. Here was a member who was, although primarily interested in the needs of his own constituents, prepared to give up sufficient time to think about the opportunities which could be tackled by the local population. Was he a man who could be trusted with the demands of a government post? Such an opportunity was soon to present itself.

Early promotion – followed swiftly by another

Shortly after Terence O'Neill became Prime Minister, the backbench member, James Chichester-Clark, was summoned to the Prime Minister's office in Parliament Buildings. He was offered the post of Assistant Government Whip and he readily accepted. This was the first step on the government ladder and an important first step on the road to a successful parliamentary career. Although it could certainly not be described as a terribly onerous task, Chichester-Clark gave its duties his full attention.

Promotion would surely come if he did a good job. And promotion did come, and much quicker than he could have anticipated. Within a month he became the government Chief Whip in succession to William Craig. Chichester-Clark was determined to show his mettle. The Chief Whip technically did not hold a Cabinet post and was only expected to be present to pick up what was going on. He was not even in fact permitted to make contributions. Notwithstanding, the new Chief Whip decided that, to do a good job, he did need to intervene and this he did regularly. 'I wasn't really supposed to say anything', he admits, 'but I felt that, when the occasion required it, I needed to ask questions and to make relevant interventions'. He often did – and O'Neill and his colleagues seemed to have no objection to their new man making useful and worthwhile contributions. From then on Chief Whips became Cabinet members. He enjoyed his job as Chief Whip above any other post he held – in truth even more than he enjoyed, or endured, as Prime Minister. In early summer 1963, James Chichester-Clark had no thoughts of attaining the first citizen post; he just wanted to get on with the job in hand.

A Chief Whip's chief occupation in the Commons was to ensure that government party Members of Parliament adhered strictly to government instructions on how to vote, especially when a three line whip was demanded. Most times Chichester-Clark's whip instructions were obeyed and members were entirely co-operative. But there were occasions when 'he could have a good row'. Sometimes his colleagues had their own interpretations of the government's policies which were not to their liking. The Chief Whip listened patiently and then told them how they were expected, as government members, to vote. Chichester-Clark knew which members were on his own wavelength and which were not and even the affable, football-loving Johnny McQuade could be brought to heel if the need arose.

In this pivotal position, Chichester-Clark was able to gauge the strengths and weaknesses of opposition members. He often wrangled with Gerry Fitt, but he always found him to be civil and never rude or unpleasant. Things were to change in the later 1960s but, in the meantime, Fitt proved a worthy political opponent. In the early and middle 1960s, Ian Paisley's name had not yet become a household one. The fiery cleric was finding his feet, a euphemistic way of describing his preparations for fire and brimstone as the years unfolded in what was soon to become the cauldron of Northern Ireland's grim 'Troubles'. In those days, however,

Chichester-Clark had little or no contact with the reverend gentleman – but his time would come, and with a vengeance.

In 1966, he added to his responsibilities as Chief Whip the post of Leader of the House. This was a largely ceremonial job which did not overly tax the member for South Londonderry. It could have been described as just another post to add to his increasingly impressive curriculum vitae. He was now a full member of the Cabinet.

A full Ministry to handle

In 1967, O'Neill called his Chief Whip to his office once more. 'I want to make you Minister of Agriculture', the Prime Minister was saying. 'Then I will be pleased to accept this new challenge' was Chichester-Clark's response. Now, as a Cabinet member, he had full and legitimate speaking rights. From the start, however, the new Minister found that he was getting advice from this one and being told exactly what to do by that one. He was required to attend one farmers' conference after another. His wife was expected to present prizes to the mothers of bonnie babies, to prettily dressed girl dancers and, most frequently of all, to ladies in Women's Institutes whose home baked cakes were their pride and joy. The Minister got on with the job, but it was not wholly to his liking.

Nonetheless he did have excellent civil servants working for him and for the interests of his Ministry. His Permanent Secretary, Mr Jimmy Young, was a fine and tremendously capable man in whom Chichester-Clark had the fullest of confidence. He was always there by his side, with answers to those interminable questions to which no Minister, no matter how great his calibre, could hold in the forefront of his mind. Young, one of Stormont's longest serving and most popular Permanent Secretaries, however, always had the right answer to give to his grateful Minister. At that time, in Stormont Castle grounds, a number of brand new civil service buildings were being erected and in one of these fine edifices (nowadays called 1960s monstrosities) the Minister of Agriculture found his new day to day working office with all his civil servants close at hand. Chichester-Clark found this a comfortable place to carry out his important work as a leading Minister in O'Neill's government. He also had his own office in Parliament Buildings where he could work and be close to the chamber should the division bells ring for a vote in the House. He could never complain about the accommodation he was given at Stormont – it was perfectly good. The work at Agriculture itself was not so much to his liking. At times he yearned to be back in the Chief Whip's office. A testing time would come in the not too distant future and he would move to another office of state far away from the oft times boring work of the Ministry of Agriculture. He remained in that job for two years until late April 1969.

A view from the constituency

Behind every good Member of Parliament there lies an equally good constituency organisation and in South Londonderry this was surely the case. The constituency chairman for most of Chichester-Clark's years as MP was Mr Ivan Wilson, a diligent and able worker for the unionist cause. At the outset, in the early days of Chichester-Clark's nomination in 1960, Wilson had not been a supporter of his candidature. He had initially been in favour of the other candidate, Mr R. A. Brown. However, when Chichester-Clark succeeded in winning the nomination, Wilson fell in behind the prospective member. And he stood behind him through thick and thin for the years to come. Never could a Member of Parliament have had such a loyal chairman. In a constituency with many local associations, Ivan Wilson and James Chichester-Clark found themselves often in each other's company at meetings in Maghera, Castledawson and in the many other South Londonderry towns and villages. Wilson remembers his MP as an 'approachable' man and certainly not a 'haughty' one. Chichester-Clark listened to anyone who wished to speak to him with the fullest attention to every detail, regardless of how insignificant might seem the issue. He spoke clearly and with assurance at meetings and rarely, if ever, resorted to 'street fighting'. Wilson describes him as a consummate member and one who readily kept in touch with his constituency officers.

In his days as Prime Minister, many local constituency meetings were difficult and could have been exacting for Chichester-Clark to handle. But he was able to deal confidently with rowdy meetings and rebellious constituents. He never held back with anything he had to say and was not afraid to deal with the many tricky issues which came up with monotonous regularity. During his premiership both chairman and member had, on more than one occasion, to 'beard rebellious associations in their dens' but the MP, on most occasions, came away with an overwhelming vote of confidence. The notion that James Chichester-Clark was a diffident and nervous man was thus soon dispelled. This 'big, decent' man was powerful as a chairman at his constituency meetings and articulate as an MP and Prime Minister at the Dispatch Box in the Commons. However, he is often remembered by the Northern Ireland population as a Prime Minister whose television delivery was, during the vital years of his premiership, strained and unconvincing.

Other civic appointments

From 1954 until 1997, a period of 43 years, James Chichester-Clark was Deputy Lieutenant and subsequently Vice Lord Lieutenant for County Londonderry. The duties were light and certainly anything but onerous in the early years and this was just as well as he was still in the army until 1960. Occasionally the Lord Lieutenant, being otherwise unavailable, would ask him to carry out some fairly minor function, which he happily performed. In later days, in the 1970s and 1980s, his duties were often more frequent and he found himself attending funerals and seeing to the niceties of welcoming Royal visitors. He recalls meeting Prince Andrew on a visit to Upperlands in the county and then dining with him in another part of his constituency. He found it almost amusing that some of Her Majesty's Lord Lieutenants sometimes wanted to share their responsibilities with their deputies and others wanted to keep all the functions to themselves. He did not aspire to this top post, so he would never know whether he would have been a sharer of jobs or a hoarder of them. The chances are, however, that he would have wanted to share the work required of Her Majesty's principal representative in his own county.

He did hold a number of what could be described as not very important chairmanships, although in truth the chief officers of those organisations would probably have considered themselves most favoured at having James Chichester-Clark, MP, as their honoured chair. If that was the case, then so be it.

7

Terence O'Neill to James Chichester-Clark: Careers and Lives So Alike

Terence Marne O'Neill was Northern Ireland's fourth Prime Minister, the predecessor to James Chichester-Clark. O'Neill was born on 10 September 1914, shortly after the outbreak of World War I, the fifth and last child of his parents. His father was, at that time, the Westminster Member of Parliament for Mid Antrim and he was, unfortunately, the first MP to be killed in action. Terence was just three months old when his father died. His maternal grandfather, Lord Houghton, had been Ireland's Viceroy in 1892, a fact of which O'Neill reminded President Eamon de Valera on a visit to Aras an Uachtarain in the early 1970s. His family, the ancient Irish family of the O'Neills, is one of the oldest traceable families in Europe. Thus was Terence O'Neill, in so many ways, destined to be a leader of modern day Irishmen.

Like Chichester-Clark, O'Neill had been at Eton and had also joined the same regiment as Chichester-Clark – the Irish Guards. Like Chichester-Clark, O'Neill had been an ADC to a Governor after the Second World War – Chichester-Clark to Earl Alexander of Tunis in Canada and O'Neill to the Governor of South Australia.

Similarities did not end there. On retirement from the army, both men had been drawn to politics. In their thirties, they both became Northern Ireland Members of Parliament, O'Neill for the County Antrim seat of Bannside, and Chichester-Clark for the County Londonderry seat of South Londonderry, just over the Bann from Bannside. Both had been returned unopposed for most of their political careers. Having to fight for their seats only came late in their respective parliamentary lives when the cold blast of sectarianism blew across Northern Ireland in the late 1960s.

There was a further link between the two men. For four years, from 1949 until 1953, Terence O'Neill was Parliamentary Secretary to Chichester-Clark's maternal grandmother, Dame Dehra Parker. For O'Neill, these were frustrating years as he felt held back when he wanted to make progress. In due course, O'Neill did gain promotion. He held various ministerial posts culminating, before his final promotion to the premiership, in the position of Minister of Finance.

Although both men rose to become Prime Minister, O'Neill was simply appointed by the then Governor, Lord Wakehurst. Like his three predecessors, there was no election for the position and, although there were many who were surprised – and even disquieted – at the selection of O'Neill, there was an immediate show of unity in support of the new Prime Minister. O'Neill had never been a constituency man and was, in large measure, unknown to the majority of the electorate. He would need to make all the running to prove himself in order to avoid early criticism. When Chichester-Clark's time came in 1969, however, he had to subject himself to a leadership election.

When O'Neill was elevated to the first citizen post, he appointed Chichester-Clark to be Chief Whip and consequently both men served in Cabinet, without a break, over the O'Neill years, 1963 until 1969. O'Neill subsequently promoted Chichester-Clark to the posts of Leader of the House (1966) and Minister of Agriculture (1967).

A reforming Prime Minister?

Lord Fitt of Bell's Hill (formerly the Stormont and Westminster MP, Gerry Fitt) described the difference between O'Neill and his predecessor, Lord Brookeborough, thus: 'Brookeborough stepped on Catholics with hob nailed boots, whereas O'Neill wore his carpet slippers'.[1] This may be history's verdict on O'Neill but, at that time in the 1960s, he was considered, by many, a reforming Prime Minister. He told the people that he wanted Catholics and Protestants to live closely together for the betterment of Northern Ireland. He made frequent overtures to the Catholic community. He was seen in Catholic schools chatting to the pupils; he was photographed with nuns in convents. This made good press in national papers, but it made O'Neill many enemies amongst the ultra

---

[1] David Gordon, *The O'Neill Years* (Belfast 1989) p. 5

Protestants. Chichester-Clark was convinced that, inwardly, O'Neill was a shy man. He found it difficult to be at ease and to speak freely even with his closest Cabinet colleagues. In a strange sort of way, O'Neill actually was more comfortable when talking to people he did not know. Chichester-Clark rightly thought that, to be Prime Minister and to be ill at ease with his colleagues, was the greatest possible disadvantage for O'Neill. There were other Cabinet colleagues, however, who thought quite the opposite and considered O'Neill to have a cosy relationship with those closest to him and to be distant, even rude, with the rank and file. Basil McIvor, a latter day supporter of O'Neill and his reforms and only elected as MP for the new constituency of Larkfield in the last days of O'Neill at the 1969 General Election, was never inspired by his Prime Minister. The fact that he was not good at mixing with the ordinary people meant that 'he did not possess the chemistry for that sort of response'.[2] Terence O'Neill was an enigma, so was he the right man for the job?

The beginnings for a new Prime Minister

Early in O'Neill's premiership, President John Kennedy was preparing for a State visit to Ireland. O'Neill considered that it would be a perfect idea to invite him to Northern Ireland to declare open the Giant's Causeway National Park. By so doing, it would dispel the myth that this Irish American President had no desire or inclination to come to Northern Ireland and meet its people. However, the Prime Minister's 'shrewd political move' was rebuffed when he was politely told that the President could not fit this visit into his busy schedule. The *Unionist* described this refusal to accept the invitation as 'Kennedy's Snub to Ulster'[3] and considered the decision as 'smacking too much of politics'. O'Neill's early ploy for a stunning coup had failed.

The Taoiseach visits Northern Ireland

Not since 1925, when W. T. Cosgrave had met Sir James Craig at the Colonial Office in London, had contact been made between the Prime

---

[2] Basil McIvor, *Hope Deferred* (Belfast 1998) p. 52
[3] *Unionist*, June 1963

Ministers of the two parts of Ireland. And so the meeting, 40 years later, was shrouded in mystery from start to finish. Terence O'Neill wanted to 'break the mould' but the method chosen was a strange way to proceed. Rather than calling his Cabinet colleagues to discuss his plan, he summoned his civil service advisors to his office and told them of his plans. He then instructed his private secretary, Jim Malley, to travel furtively to Dublin to deliver the invitation to Sean Lemass through the Taoiseach's head of the Ministry of Finance, Ken Whitaker. Lemass gladly accepted the invitation, with only a passing mention to his Cabinet members. The visit took place on 14 January 1965.

But the auguries for the visit were not good. The previous night severe storms caused havoc in the Province. Two large ships, 'The Royal Ulsterman' and the oil carrier 'British Victory', collided in Belfast Lough and the recently built, 2 year old St Brendan's church in Sydenham, a suburb of East Belfast, collapsed.

When Lemass arrived in his ministerial limousine, he was greeted by O'Neill, alone of the Northern Ireland government. Shamefaced and embarrassed Ministers, including James Chichester-Clark, were simply summoned to take lunch with the Taoiseach. Brian Faulkner's immediate response was succinct – 'You must be joking'.[4] The Cabinet Ministers were not best pleased but, apart from Harry West who refused to come, they did partake of lunch with Lemass as required and requested. Soon afterwards, however, in the quiet and secrecy of the Cabinet room, they made known their great displeasure to the Prime Minister. To be simply informed of such a historic event showed, in Faulkner's words, a 'lack of trust'. Such a 'cloak and dagger' visit could only invite suspicion. Thereafter, support from the Ulster Unionist Party began to slip away from O'Neill. However, shortly afterwards, the Ulster Unionist Party did pass a vote of confidence in the Prime Minister at a meeting in that cockpit of Ulster unionism, the Sandy Row Orange Hall.

Yet, throughout the island of Ireland, the visit was almost uniformly welcomed. Politicians from all the parties, unionist and Opposition alike, expressed their pleasure at this historic event. Even the head of the Orange Order, Sir George Clark, supported the move. In the morning newspapers in Belfast, he was reported as saying 'that any meeting of this nature between Heads of State was both desirable and

---

[4] Brian Faulkner, *Memoirs of a Statesman* (London 1978) p. 39

necessary when both sides could benefit mutually'.[5] This was praise indeed. Entirely predictably, the lone voice of dissent came from the Reverend Ian Paisley who accused O'Neill of nothing short of treachery.

To Chichester-Clark, this visit made a great deal of sense. He realised that O'Neill thought he would be universally unpopular for arranging such a visit but Chichester-Clark soon made it clear to his Prime Minister that he, as Chief Whip, was not at all 'put out' by the invitation to Lemass. He told O'Neill he considered the relations between north and south had to be strengthened and that 'we needed to be at peace' with our southern neighbours. It was necessary for O'Neill to know that most of his colleagues were behind him, although most of their initial reactions were rather cool when the visit was sprung on them, offending a number of sensitive feelings.

The symbolism of this visit was obvious. The ice had been broken. Former Taoisigh and Prime Ministers like de Valera, Craig and Brookeborough could never have considered it. O'Neill and Lemass (himself an active insurgent in the 1916 Easter Rising) felt the time was as right as it could ever be. O'Neill told Lemass that the visit would probably do him harm. It certainly did; yet for Lemass the visit proved a vital contribution to his success in the General Election which took place in the Republic later that year. He saw it as 'a potent symbolism'.[6]

Ill-conceived decisions

Since the inception of the Northern Irish state, there has always existed an east/west split. Geographically, the river Bann, which runs north/south through the Province, has effectively been the dividing line. The majority of the population who live to the west are Catholic and those to the east are largely Protestant. Politically, therefore, nationalism has ever held sway in the west, and unionism in the east. In the days of the foundation of the state in 1921, when people like Edward Carson had been opposed to splitting the ancient Province of Ulster for political expediency, the predominately Catholic counties of Cavan, Monaghan and Donegal were adjudged too unsafe to hold within the new Northern Ireland state. There is some logic, however misguided it may seem, that those west of the Bann

---

[5] *News Letter,* 15 January 1965

[6] Michael O'Sullivan, *Sean Lemass – a Biography* (Dublin 1994) p. 179

have always considered themselves captives in the northern state. And successive unionist Prime Ministers, including Terence O'Neill, took little heed of the reality of the situation. They were not able to comprehend, or simply chose to ignore, the reasons why those in the west seemed ill at ease with the status quo.

Terence O'Neill, ostensibly the reforming and moderate Prime Minister, fell into the trap when he made two significant faux pas during 1966. He supported the Lockwood Commission's recommendation that Northern Ireland's second university should be sited, on a green field site, in the predominately Protestant town of Coleraine. Coleraine lies east of the Bann – just. This seemed an unfortunate choice of location, for a number of reasons. That the campus was to be built on an entirely new site in a Protestant town east of the Bann would clearly antagonise the minority population. In Londonderry – the Province's second city and itself firmly situated west of the Bann – there already was a well established educational foundation, Magee College, which, although nominally a Presbyterian college, was accommodating students of every religious persuasion and of none. Most people in Northern Ireland thought O'Neill had – to use an Ulster phrase – 'taken the head staggers'. They wondered how a reforming Prime Minister could take such a decision. When they protested, they were ignored by the Cabinet, which included James Chichester-Clark who lived and farmed west of the Bann, but who declared in favour of the Coleraine site. There were ominous voices, too, which did not want to see expansion of any kind in Londonderry. To ultra loyalists it was anathema to bring a new university or even additional industry to the maiden city. This would mean that these jobs and positions of influence and power would surely go to the minority population, swamping the Protestant hegemony in the city.

Terence O'Neill and his Cabinet endorsed another amazing decision in that same year. The Wilson Committee, headed by Professor Tom Wilson, prepared a plan and blueprint for the future of Northern Ireland, which included the building of more homes, the construction of motorways and the upgrading of the entire Northern Ireland infrastructure. He concluded that there ought to be a new city. This was a sound idea but when the proposal was made that this city should be situated to include the towns of Portadown and Lurgan, east of the Bann, there was uproar. If great was the clamour at its proposed location, even greater was the deafening roar and cries of utter disbelief when the name of the city was to be Craigavon, after the Province's very loyal and unionist first Prime Minister, James Craig, Lord Craigavon. Insensitivity – show thyself. Terence O'Neill proceeded to agree to this too. He could not see, or did not want to see, what all the fuss was about. History's subsequent verdict on the city of Craigavon was unfavourable. It never got off its feet. Nor did the locals from Lurgan and Portadown ever warm to their new-found notoriety. They would far rather have remained just the two anonymous and quiet towns which they had always been.

More trouble ahead

With the British Prime Minister, Harold Wilson, now breathing down his neck and insisting on speedy reforms, O'Neill proceeded apace to effect changes. Londonderry Corporation was to be abolished and a Londonderry Development Commission put in its place. The blatant inequalities in the allocation of public housing throughout Northern Ireland, and especially in the west, brought about a central Housing Authority, which was later to become the Housing Executive. An Ombudsman was to be speedily introduced to listen to complaints and a proposal to have 'one man, one vote' for local government elections was to be put on the statute book without further ado. Although O'Neill was seen as the facilitator of these reforms, it could be argued that Wilson's pressure had actually brought them about. But, at this critical juncture in November 1968, the Chichester-Clark brothers made an extremely valuable contribution to the reform debate. Realising that O'Neill needed some further encouragement to proceed with reforms which he had thought politically impossible at the time, James and Robin quickly noted down the ideas which they considered to be of great importance and called O'Neill to join them to discuss their points. In the subsequent, somewhat informal, meeting, O'Neill was persuaded to proceed with an accelerated rate of reform as proposed by the Chichester-Clark duo. O'Neill genuinely wanted changes to make the Catholic people more accepting of the Northern Ireland constitution whilst Wilson wanted to keep up the pressure on O'Neill and his Cabinet colleagues. In truth, however, there is little doubt that Terence O'Neill found the pressure unbearable and caved in to the reform demands of the increasingly vociferous minority. Harold Wilson was never a popular man with unionists, either within its hierarchy or its rank and file. There were constant jibes aimed at the British Prime Minister and unionist newspapers were filled, week after week, with perceptively cutting cartoons poking fun at him.

By this time, too, midway through his years of premiership, the berating chants of Ian Paisley and other radical Protestants started to cause further stress for O'Neill. These individuals were now raising the age old fears that reform meant nothing short of 'Rome rule' from the south of Ireland. They orchestrated their forces cleverly and many who had thought that O'Neill's proposed changes were worthy of consideration, were now having second thoughts. Pressure was on them to conform to the unionist sectarian ideology. The Prime Minister, ominously, was becoming obsessed with Paisley's antics.

This mid year of his premiership was 1966, and was the year of the 50th anniversary of the Easter Rising in Dublin. O'Neill and his government were aware of the possibility of unrest on the streets and they took precautions to ensure that there would be no disturbances. As it transpired, there were no real problems, but not long afterwards Paisley and his supporters picketed the meeting of the Presbyterian General Assembly in Belfast. As the Governor, the Presbyterian Lord Erskine, and his wife, were coming out of the building, they were subjected to much verbal abuse and aggressive jostling. This episode adversely affected Lady Erskine's health and the majority of decent Ulstermen and women were indignant that such a disgraceful occurrence should have happened. Paisley was sent to jail in connection with these disturbances. However, rather than doing a service to O'Neill and the moderate majority, the outcome proved to be 'food and drink' to Paisley and his followers. Ulster's extreme Protestants like nothing better than a good Protestant martyr and there was none better than Ian Paisley. O'Neill, although he received wholehearted support from all shades of public opinion and from the press, was finding it difficult to retain the momentum of a reforming premier. And, although the speeches at the 12th of July parades trumpeted 'clear and unequivocal' backing for O'Neill, the first anti-O'Neill graffiti began to appear on street walls.

By September a revolt was brewing amongst a number of dissident unionist MPs, including Boal, Warnock, McQuade and Nixon. They had not been able to forgive O'Neill for allowing the Easter Rising demonstrations back in April and they were determined to make life difficult for the Prime Minister. They even approached Lord Brookeborough to ascertain if he would be prepared to act as a caretaker Prime Minister, but he declared himself 'too old and too square' for the job. In the event, O'Neill acted decisively and, after a critical meeting on 27 September 1966, the press announced that the revolt had petered out. It was the Chief Whip, James Chichester-Clark, who had brought together a number of prominent MPs and Cabinet Ministers to consider the best possible ways of supporting the Prime Minister. Significantly this 'back the government' group met on at least three occasions, evidence, if such was needed, of the concern of many that O'Neill's days might be numbered. However support for O'Neill flowed in from all sources, enabling Chichester-Clark to boldly announce that the crisis was over. The dissidents had been crushed but, as would be seen in due course, not totally bowed down.

Although O'Neill continued to make visits abroad during 1967 and 1968 spelling out the real benefits of investment in Northern Ireland – and much new industry did come to the Province at this time – the embryonic Civil Rights Movement was now shaping up to oppose the government. They decided to take to the streets. Their first march was in Dungannon, followed by one in Londonderry on 5 October 1968. In the disturbances during this march, many of the marchers, including Gerry Fitt MP, were batoned by the police, resulting in several injuries and a number of arrests. The Home Affairs Minister, William Craig, was continuously criticised for his right wing attitudes and for his handling of the Londonderry parade. O'Neill could no longer stomach his actions and, in December, sacked Craig from his post.

At this critical time, the most notorious Civil Rights incident took place at Burntollet Bridge outside Londonderry on the fourth and last day of a march from Belfast to the maiden city which had commenced on 1 January 1969. Here the marchers were ambushed by stone throwing hooligans whose numbers, it later transpired, included a number of the Ulster Special Constabulary (USC), the 'B' Specials, in civilian clothes. This further exacerbated the difficulties for O'Neill and his Cabinet. The fact that members of the RUC had been involved added fuel to the fire. The Cabinet members, including Chichester-Clark, seemed to have had no idea how disenchanted the minority population had become. Such a myopic view seemed to encapsulate the inability of mainstream Ulster Unionism to understand the strength of feeling for real reform amongst a large percentage of the minority Northern Ireland population. Yet more seeds of discontent had now been strewn across the highways and byways of the Province and the Cabinet remained oblivious of the ever growing unease which surrounded them.

The report by Lord Cameron, which had been commissioned by O'Neill, placed the blame for the disturbances upon the police, the forces of law and order and on the poorly marshalled demonstrators. There had been no hiding place from the prying eyes of the television cameras. The horrific scenes were broadcast throughout the United Kingdom and further afield. The image of the police had been seriously tarnished. Terence O'Neill then did what he himself liked to do best. He appeared on television to appeal to the better nature of the ordinary men and women of Northern Ireland. He received an overwhelming groundswell of support when over 150,000 people sent in newspaper coupons printed in the local press with the demand to 'keep O'Neill at the wheel'. But O'Neill had miscalculated. He was tricked by this massive vote of confidence. Shortly afterwards, Brian Faulkner, for so long the hard working Minister of Commerce, yet one who had never given his unequivocal support to O'Neill, informed the Prime Minister that he had not agreed with the setting up of the Cameron Commission and had no option but to leave the government. There followed acrimonious correspondence between Faulkner and O'Neill. When it came into the public domain, it finally brought their mutual dislike for one another out into the open. There was no turning back and, although O'Neill would dearly have loved him not to have taken this drastic step, he could not change the mind of the ambitious Faulkner. To add to his woes, O'Neill's Minister of Health, William Morgan – never a fervent O'Neill supporter – also resigned.

While O'Neill had been insisting that he would not go to the country, he decided to do just that. He announced a general election for 24 February 1969. This 'Crossroads Election' was a political gamble which failed. Cabinet colleagues were generally against O'Neill's move, including Chichester-Clark. They felt that he had been misled by the seeming enthusiasm of the population and that things were too uncertain to go to the polls. Although they would almost certainly win the election, the auguries for a really positive result were not good. And so it transpired. O'Neill did win the election, but too many of his fellow 'pro-O'Neill' Unionist MPs were opposed; by anti-O'Neill candidates, by some of Ian Paisley's faction, or by young Civil Rights candidates. In his own constituency of Bannside, O'Neill was opposed by both Ian Paisley and the Civil Rights leader, Michael Farrell. O'Neill, in this his first contested election since becoming the member for Bannside 23 years earlier, won by just 1,414 votes over a jubilant and vociferous Paisley. (It was not to be long before Paisley did win the seat). O'Neill was hurt, dejected and disappointed.

In this election, Chichester-Clark was opposed for the unionist nomination in South Londonderry by William Douglas, a vote which he only narrowly won. Douglas' intervention could have had serious implications for the sitting member. The *Mid Ulster Mail* of 15 February 1969 reported on the nomination meeting which had been held at Maghera Orange Hall on 12 February 'he [Chichester-Clark] had a two to one majority over his anti-O'Neill opponent, Mr William Douglas, an ex-Flight Lieutenant from Dungiven. The actual voting figures were – Major Chichester-Clark 258 (subsequently amended to the correct figure of 138), Mr Douglas 74'.[7] In the election proper, and for the first time in his parliamentary career, he had a contest on his hands. He was opposed by the up and coming Bernadette Devlin and, although he did win, he did so by just a little over 3,000 votes. Significantly, throughout the election campaign, Chichester-Clark had made little or no mention of Terence O'Neill nor his support or otherwise for him. The election had been a scare for O'Neill in particular and for the Ulster Unionists in general. Chichester-Clark, too, breathed a sigh of relief.

Heading for disaster

The RUC, with just 3,000 personnel, was now becoming increasingly over-stretched. The members of the force were exhausted. Some now had to be away from home for up to four days. Worse was to come. In April 1969, bombs severely damaged water and electricity installations. (This turned out to be a subversive act perpetrated not, as initially declared, by elements of the IRA, but by Protestant extremists). The sight of queues of people lining up to obtain drinking water from standpipes was reminiscent of wartime. The police had not been in a position to protect these locations and so O'Neill reluctantly called in the army to undertake the task of guarding these vital supplies. The police, and the government, were clearly losing their grip on the situation. And, to add insult to injury, Bernadette Devlin romped home with a comfortable majority of 4,211 votes over the Ulster Unionist, Mrs Anna Forrest, in a Westminster by-election in Mid Ulster on 17 April. The poll had been occasioned by the death of the sitting Ulster Unionist member, George Forrest. Devlin had become the youngest MP at Westminster.

---

[7] *Mid Ulster Mail,* 15 February 1969

O'Neill, however, was not finished. He could clearly see that 'the writing was on the wall', but even so, he pushed ahead with more reform. In April, after lengthy, heated debates in the Stormont Commons chamber, he eventually put through the 'one man, one vote' legislation. Amongst his own parliamentary party, both MPs and Senators, he was only successful in his endeavours by the slimmest of majorities – 28 votes to 22 – and it was in this division that Chichester-Clark showed his colours. He did not, in the end, support O'Neill and voted against the proposal. He may not have agreed with the timing of this particular reform and was not opposed to the principle of universal franchise, but stated; 'I question, firstly, whether this concession at this time will stop the activities in the streets and, secondly, I fear that our supporters will lose all faith in the determination of the present government'.[8] Furthermore, he declared that he had resigned to prevent any public 'slanging match' between O'Neill and himself.

The day after the debate, he resigned as Minister of Agriculture. He contended that O'Neill had, in fact, encouraged him to put his hat in the ring for the premiership. His constituency chairman had similarly thrust his MP forward believing him to be the right man for the job and his brother, the Westminster member for Londonderry, Robin Chichester-Clark, added his weight to ensure that James sought the top job.

James Chichester-Clark, hitherto virtually unknown to the general public of Northern Ireland, was now catapulted into view. Had he really the intention of gaining the top job if O'Neill was toppled? Did he seek the post out of loyalty to the Province? The Agriculture Minister's resignation sent shock waves throughout the party. And, by the end of that week in April 1969, Terence O'Neill had resigned as Prime Minister for Northern Ireland.

Terence O'Neill had been Prime Minister for over six years and, as he intoned to his television audience, he had done all he could for the Province. He had felt that the fact that his name was O'Neill should have been an asset in his ambitions, but this proved not to be the case. He never had the 'common touch'. He was still an aloof member of the gentry. His speeches, whilst often genuine enough, were wooden, and his manner, however hard he tried, was stilted. Chichester-Clark had often spent time with O'Neill, particularly in the recent past, to get the Prime Minister to mingle again with people and his Cabinet colleagues. O'Neill had become so obsessed with Paisley and his manoeuvres that he seemed no longer

---

[8] *Irish News*, 24 April 1969

capable of dealing rationally with even his closest supporters. In those last days he had become a complete isolate, despite Chichester-Clark's best efforts to bring him to his senses.

After handing his resignation to the Governor, Lord Grey, O'Neill went back to vote in the succession stakes. The candidates were Chichester-Clark and Brian Faulkner. O'Neill voted for Chichester-Clark, who had surely brought about his final downfall, and it was Chichester-Clark who won by a single vote – 17 to 16. O'Neill said, in his autobiography, of Chichester-Clark: 'I don't think, though, that he had any idea of what he was in for'.[9] He also described his successor as a man 'with a very unpolitical mind'.[10] Faulkner, too, had his own ideas as to why he lost the election. In his *Memoirs of a Statesman* he states that 'there were many, like myself, who thought it was a scheme arranged between them to ensure that power was kept in the hands of the 'Big House'. Chichester-Clark…was unknown and inexperienced'.[11] David Gordon, in his book *The O'Neill Years,* is damning in his estimation of James Chichester-Clark. He calls his election thus: 'It must go down as one of the stupidest decisions ever reached in the history of politics. By passing over Faulkner, the Unionist Party effectively sealed its fate'.[12] Owen Dudley Edwards puts another slant on the matter; 'Terence O'Neill ultimately found himself faced with a whole host violently competing with one another for the honour of assassinating him. Messrs Craig, Faulkner, Morgan and James Chichester-Clark led four separate revolts'.[13] But Chichester-Clark it was who had won the race. Time would now tell which prophecy or opinion would prevail.

The story behind that resignation

The truth of Chichester-Clark's resignation was in this wise. Throughout O'Neill's years as Prime Minister, Chichester-Clark had always remained faithful to his colleague. After all, since 1963, Chichester-Clark had been

---

[9] Terence O'Neill, *The Autobiography of Terence O'Neill* (London 1972) p. 127

[10] *Ibid.,* p. 129

[11] Brian Faulkner, *Memoirs of a Statesman* (London 1978) p. 54

[12] David Gordon, *The O'Neill Years* (Belfast 1989) pp. 155 and 156

[13] Owen Dudley Edwards, *The Sins of Our Fathers* (Dublin 1970) p. 17

appointed to positions of some importance in the government. He had been Chief Whip and Leader of the House and such was O'Neill's confidence in him, that he appointed him to the Ministry of Agriculture in 1967. These did not seem the actions of a person who was distrusting of his proposed appointee. Chichester-Clark was a loyal supporter of O'Neill policies. But where did things go wrong, culminating in a resignation just a week before O'Neill quit his post?

We must remind ourselves of the state of affairs in Northern Ireland at that time. The reforms being advocated were unanimously supported by those from whom such unequivocal support could be expected. There was plenty of support from the churches and also from many public bodies who saw the necessity to have the reforms to ensure the future of their businesses. The Catholic population was steeling itself to believe that, at last, a unionist Prime Minister was about to bring a more democratic society to Northern Ireland. Hard-line unionists, however, were not so optimistic and hopeful but were apprehensive and extremely sceptical of the proposed reforms. There was, for example, downright opposition from William Craig and his cohorts who continued to talk in emotive and irrational terms about O'Neill's reforms. Where did James Chichester-Clark stand at these crossroads?

The events of the week of 19 to 26 April 1969 throw some light on the situation. On Saturday 19 April, there was a full Cabinet meeting at Stormont when it was agreed that the 'one man, one vote' proposal would be supported. The vote was unanimous. In that company was Chichester-Clark, who must have voted for the reform. On the following Tuesday, 22 April, there was a noisy and argumentative party meeting, involving all unionist members as well as their colleagues from the Senate. Many spoke in favour of the reforms, but there were others who spoke vociferously against them. The meeting went on and on. The atmosphere was electric. The reform measures were in the balance. O'Neill threatened to resign if he was not given an endorsement to his proposals. The meeting was obviously not going to be finished that evening and it was decided to continue the discussion the next day. O'Neill, realising that it was late and knowing that he would have a long journey home, offered Chichester-Clark a bed for the night at Stormont Castle. Although initially agreeing to take up the offer, Chichester-Clark then declined and made his way back home in his official car. O'Neill was, by now, having concerns about the way that Chichester-Clark was likely to vote and so he was pleased to hear 'on the grapevine' that his Agriculture Minister was going to support him.

But why was he concerned? Surely Chichester-Clark had backed him at the Cabinet meeting the previous Saturday? O'Neill must have had reason to suspect that his distant clansman was wavering in his support for this reform. His fears proved to have foundation.

In his autobiography, Terence O'Neill states that Chichester-Clark 'looked a worried man'[14] on his return to Stormont the next morning. O'Neill's fears about Chichester-Clark's support were soon realised. In a brief impromptu meeting, Chichester-Clark informed the Prime Minister that he could not fully support him. O'Neill then supposed that Chichester-Clark would abstain from the vote, only to be devastated by the discovery that he would be voting against him. O'Neill was dumbfounded and considered that his Agriculture Minister had been 'nobbled'. In the eventual vote, O'Neill got the support of his colleagues, but only by those 28 votes to 22.

Chichester-Clark promptly resigned his post, leaving O'Neill in the lurch. The Prime Minister could surely not survive much longer himself. In his letter of resignation to O'Neill, Chichester-Clark declared that he was sorry to be leaving the administration which he had happily served for some years. He said that it was not that he did not approve of the universal franchise reforms, but he felt that the timing was not right. In all likelihood, O'Neill did not believe this excuse. An editorial in the *Irish Times* of 24 April 1969 ascribed Chichester-Clark's protestations of his belief in the principles of 'one man, one vote' and his doubt about the timing as 'grossly insulting to the intelligence of the people'.[15] Others were equally sceptical of Chichester-Clark's motives. J. J. Lee considers that 'Chichester-Clark's resignation might have been in collusion with O'Neill',[16] and Brian Faulkner believed that it was nothing more than an ascendancy plot.

The truth is more difficult to discover. It is true that Chichester-Clark's resignation at this critical time certainly thrust his name into the headlines and into the public eye. This was vital for one who had never been a very prominent member of O'Neill's government. Nor did he have any obvious popular support in many parts of the Province. He was rather an unknown quantity to most people.

The timing of his resignation was crucial. Chichester-Clark took this step exactly at the time when everyone's eyes were firmly on O'Neill

---

[14] Terence O'Neill, *The Autobiography of Terence O'Neill* (London 1972) p. 125
[15] *Irish Times,* 24 April 1969
[16] J.J. Lee, *Ireland 1912-1985* (Cambridge 1989) p. 424

and whether or not he would succeed in bringing about his reforms. Then came this bombshell. His faithful colleague, on a rather flimsy excuse, had chosen this time – of all times – to abandon the ship of state. Chichester-Clark's decision to resign rather took the other MPs' 'eyes off the ball'. When asked two days later by a reporter from the *Belfast Telegraph* whether he was now a contender for the premiership if O'Neill were to resign (which now seemed probable rather than possible), Chichester-Clark said 'Good Lord, no. I have never thought of it at all'.[17] This is hard to believe. He must have known that more and more of the unionist MPs, even O'Neill's supporters, knew that the Prime Minister was likely to resign soon. He now felt sure that O'Neill's supporters would vote for him if he put his name forward, for they certainly did not want Brian Faulkner to succeed. Their cry sounded abroad 'Anyone but Faulkner!' James Chichester-Clark was certainly not so naïve as not to realise that there would shortly be a fight to succeed O'Neill. He was convinced that he had a chance to take on what many would consider the worst poisoned chalice of all – the post of Prime Minister of Northern Ireland. In less than a week, he had realised this ambition. He had the chalice securely grasped in his hand.

The lull before the storm: a chance to reflect

The premiership of James Chichester-Clark, whilst seen by so many as being an unimportant and insignificant interlude, was, in truth, the most critical episode in the sorry state of affairs in Northern Ireland. It has been important, therefore, to take time to reflect on the influence of Terence O'Neill's six years in power upon the 689 days which were to be the duration of his successor as Prime Minister, James Chichester-Clark.

Chichester-Clark was a Cabinet member from 1963 until 1969, but one who could never have been described as mainstream. He sat, for most of the time, on the edge of the dissension and mayhem which oftentimes gripped his colleagues. We must consider O'Neill's obvious shortcomings. Others have written a great deal on what they thought of Terence O'Neill, but objective articles and even biographies are thin on the ground. For a long time, the only books on O'Neill were his own autobiography, published in 1972, and a volume of his speeches, entitled *Ulster at the*

---

[17] *Belfast Telegraph*, 25 April 1969

Crossroads, introduced by John Cole, dated 1969. In 1989, David Gordon published his polemic, *The O'Neill Years*. It is not my intention to add to the O'Neill writings, but it is essential that sufficient is said on his premiership to show the effects on the two years in power of his successor. Gordon presents the view that O'Neill was a disaster for Northern Ireland. He describes him as being patronising to the Catholic minority; he cites his wanderings throughout the world as 'self aggrandisement'; he scoffs in his description of Northern Ireland as 'a sovereign state'. In short, he adjudges O'Neill to have been too full of his own importance and never in the slightest way interested in bringing Catholics into any sort of sharing of power. He often quotes the phrase 'Croppies lie down' – a reference to the fact that the Catholic population ought to have been happy to continue to be under the unionist jackboot, especially when they were being thrown some fairly inconsequential reform measures. On the other hand, O'Neill himself seemed convinced that his approaches to the Catholic schools and his proffering a hand of friendship towards the southern Taoiseach were evidence sufficient to show his calibre as a premier worthy of support from all the citizens of Northern Ireland. He spoke long and often about the improvement in employment and housing for all those in the Province willing to support the government. He pleaded and beseeched everyone to follow his lead and keep Northern Ireland ahead of all the other regions of the United Kingdom. He engaged in his Programme to Enlist the People campaign and in his Civic Weeks as his way of encouraging both communities to live amicably together.

But there are some unquestionable points which cannot be forgotten in O'Neill's premiership. Until 1965, O'Neill was making slow and steady progress. This was the time when, if he was genuinely interested in the minority population, he could have brought them into positions of some prominence. He could have taken the opportunity to improve their lot in housing and to bring the archaic local government franchise into line. This would not have done anything to undermine his in-built unionist majority at Stormont, for it would have shown that he was prepared to break down the unionist hegemony. But O'Neill chose to do nothing at all. In the general election that year, he grasped his chance to smash the Northern Ireland Labour Party (NILP), a party which had done remarkably well in the previous general election. Why, then, did he want to emasculate a party which was in favour of the union with Great Britain? He saw the NILP as a threat to the overall power of the Ulster Unionists, especially in Belfast. And so he set about destroying them politically – and he succeeded. The NILP was reduced to just two seats at Stormont. Many saw in O'Neill, at this time, a steely and almost frightening determination to extinguish his opponents. He cunningly displayed his real ambition – to ensure the continuance of one party unionist rule. He was powerful in 1965.

Then the cracks began to appear. 1966 was his annus horribilis and perhaps the beginning of the end for him. He was often asked about Catholics joining the Ulster Unionist Party and, on the face of it, he thought this a good thing. But he never did anything to encourage this and the perfect exemplification of this happened in early 1969 just before his 'Crossroads Election'. Louis Boyle, who was very involved in unionist politics and himself a Catholic, sought the unionist nomination for South Down. He had excellent credentials and widespread support from party activists and friends in his home constituency. But the local party officials decided not to run a candidate, even though Boyle had indicated that he wanted to stand and felt that he had a reasonable chance of attracting both Catholic and Protestant voters. Seeing that he was getting nowhere in Newry, he appealed to the Prime Minister. His pleadings fell on deaf ears. O'Neill did not seem to be interested in supporting Boyle. Although the affair may have exercised O'Neill's mind for some time he cited, as his excuse, the convention that Headquarters and the Prime Minister never interfered with local party decisions. Many senior unionists, including his successor, considered that the party had missed an excellent chance to move forward. Soon afterwards, Boyle resigned from the unionist party, having been thwarted in his endeavours. Gone was O'Neill's chance to improve the lot of Catholic unionists if, in fact, he ever genuinely wanted to. The truth is that he never could see Catholics in any position of power in the Party. Having Catholic unionist MPs was anathema to him.

His government continued to delude itself. There were even those in the party who seriously believed that the Northern Ireland government could break away from parity with Great Britain. Perhaps the Province could aspire to independence. Although O'Neill himself had no truck with talk of UDI, he probably had ideas above his station. However, wiser counsel prevailed in the guise of Herbert Kirk, the Minister of Finance, who reminded these devolutionists that it was the British government which held the real power – and the purse strings.

When confronted by the Civil Rights campaigners, O'Neill clearly went in the wrong direction. Predictably, one might say, he became negative and defensive, rather than taking the opportunity to meet with them and discuss their points of view. But, realistically, this would have been impossible for a unionist Prime Minister of O'Neill's calibre. He was only interested in offering crumbs from the master's table to those who eschewed change in the status quo.

David Gordon, in his book, appears to think seriously that a truly reformist Prime Minister and unionist government could have, in effect, done away with Stormont. This is hardly likely or realistic. However it should have been possible for latter day unionist 'forward thinkers' (I dislike the word 'moderate' in this circumstance) like Basil McIvor, Anne Dickson and Robin Bailie, to have pushed their views to make positive changes in involving the minority – and many of the majority too – in a more embracing type of administration. The chances were certainly not taken, and Terence O'Neill resigned leaving his two successors with much to do.

When Lord Brookeborough eventually resigned in March 1963, he had been Prime Minister for just short of twenty years. He was nearly 75 years old. He was too old to be an effective Prime Minister – this was obvious and plain to see. He attended Stormont on only one day per week and Chichester-Clark, and most others, were relieved to hear that the former premier had at last handed in his resignation to Lord Wakehurst, the Governor. They were not sorry to see him go and concluded that Brookeborough had not taken his own advice about staying in the job too long. Brookeborough had always protested that Craigavon had overstayed his term as Prime Minister. Yet the Colebrooke squire was four years older than Craigavon when he eventually resigned.

And when the Governor summoned Terence O'Neill to Hillsborough to offer him the Prime Minister's portfolio, no one was really surprised. Some thought it odd that Brookeborough had not pushed his friends Lord Glentoran or John Andrews, for they knew that Terence O'Neill was never his favourite. Yet it was rather assumed that O'Neill, having the greater political brain, would get the job.

In those days before elections for the post of Prime Minister at Stormont, there was little any Member of Parliament could do to influence the decision. And so Chichester-Clark, like his colleagues, simply accepted it. Although O'Neill was not a socialite, he would be a great improvement on the ageing Lord Brookeborough. O'Neill was not popular and had only a limited circle of friends and he eventually came to rely, almost exclusively, on his private secretary, Jim Malley. O'Neill had never been easy to approach, in total contrast to his predecessor, and Chichester-Clark, from his earliest days as Chief Whip, had to do much to push and drive O'Neill. Being in this privileged position, he could interrupt the Prime Minister when the need arose.

Chichester-Clark, by his own admission, tended to be a cautious man, and that made O'Neill cautious too. When O'Neill started to visit Catholic schools, Chichester-Clark counselled him to go slowly, for he knew that trouble would loom from those in the party who were not keen to see such moves. O'Neill did not always take his advice, but there is evidence that Chichester-Clark often freely offered it. In Cabinet the two men worked closely together and Chichester-Clark, for the most part, supported the Prime Minister. When Lemass visited Stormont in January 1965, Chichester-Clark considered the action wise and timely. When the new university was announced for the Coleraine site, and not the Magee site, he gave O'Neill his full support. He had nothing to say on the choice of Craigavon as the new city and did what he could to pour oil on troubled waters following the public outcry. When Harry West was sacked by O'Neill, Chichester-Clark thought the decision absolutely correct and considered West to have been very foolish.

James Chichester-Clark may have been a modest man. Some may have said that he had little political nous. Others may have scorned the Major as being a lightweight. Yet, when the time came, it was he who became Prime Minister of Northern Ireland. He felt that he was the man for the job, regardless of what he said in public. He knew O'Neill's days were numbered. He could not stomach Brian Faulkner getting the job. And so he made his move. His excuse in resigning over the timing of 'one man, one vote' was a ploy. He moved into the post with almost military precision – he had the enemy cornered and, while the attention was focused on O'Neill, he quickly moved to outflank his rival, Faulkner. He took on the position rather more confidently than he declared. He had assumed the mantle as Northern Ireland's fifth Prime Minister.

8

Early Days of Premiership

Election as Prime Minister

On the day following Chichester-Clark's elevation, the *Guardian* described his election as leader as a 'kind of posthumous victory for the policies of Captain O'Neill'.[1] Owen Dudley Edwards made the point that 'his [Chichester-Clark's] chief claim to fame to date being his luck in having hit on the proper timing for leaving the sinking O'Neill ship'.[2] Jonathan Bardon declared; 'The parliamentary Unionist Party, by a margin of one vote, chose a safe, compromise candidate as prime minister, Major James Chichester-Clark'.[3] Rather disingenuously, F. S. L. Lyons in his *Ireland since the Famine* thought his chances of success as follows; 'But Major Chichester-Clark, apart from his habitual air of shambling bewilderment, as of an amateur fallen among professionals, never had the remotest chance of dominating his party'.[4] Which, then, of these prognostications would prove to be the case.

Seeking unanimity

As soon as the result had been announced, and those involved had taken in just how close the vote had been, the members of the Parliamentary Ulster Unionist Party took immediate steps to unanimously endorse the election

---

[1] *The Guardian,* 2 May 1969
[2] Owen Dudley Edwards, *The Sins of Our Fathers* (Dublin 1970) p. 38
[3] Jonathan Bardon, *A History of Ulster* (Belfast 1992) p. 665
[4] F. S. L. Lyons, *Ireland since the Famine* (London, 1973) p. 765

of Chichester-Clark. He had fully expected, as had Roy Bradford the Chief Whip who had been in charge of his campaign, to win more convincingly than by that single vote, 17 to 16. It was later suspected that Captain William Long and Nat Minford had changed sides to vote for Faulkner. Two of the most forthright opponents of Chichester-Clark in the election stakes – John Brooke and Desmond Boal – at once took the bull by the horns and proposed and seconded unanimous acceptance of James Chichester-Clark as leader and Prime Minister. This proposal was passed with acclamation and the first hurdle of his premiership had been surmounted.

The speed of the proposal was seen as a way of ensuring a unified front when the new Prime Minister would present himself to the people. It would have been most undignified, to say the least, to have the public witness a divided and discordant group of Ulster Unionist MPs emerging from Stormont. There were those, however, who did not consider that the 17-16 majority was evidence of a split in the unionist ranks. On the contrary, Commander A. W. Anderson, MP for Londonderry, confidently suggested that 'we were trying to decide a very difficult decision between two excellent men. Major Chichester-Clark and Mr Brian Faulkner impressed the Party tremendously'.[5] For his own part, Chichester-Clark sounded upbeat and confident. 'What I have to do now is gain the trust of the country. I am going all out for that with the help of my colleagues. The safety and security of Northern Ireland is my first charge'.[6]

How to form a Cabinet and not offend

Now in the unenviable position of Prime Minister, James Chichester-Clark set about selecting a Cabinet. He realised that his choice was limited, but dared not delay his decisions, realising that the appointments he had to make would be vital. On the Saturday following his election and in the seclusion of his new office at Stormont, he spent time considering who should be in his Cabinet. He knew he could afford no mistakes, for he had to satisfy the various divergent strands of unionism. In the end, his choice was widely acknowledged as having been a reasonably wise one. He included many of Terence O'Neill's former men and he introduced others who represented the more right wing faction. Although there were

[5] *Londonderry Sentinel,* 7 May 1969
[6] *Daily Mirror,* 2 May 1969

rumblings of discontent, his attempt at 'bridge building' was seen as a fair reflection of his moderate stance in setting up his administration.

He clearly wanted to broaden his government. Consequently, he brought in four of his leading critics. He offered Brian Faulkner the post of Minister of Development. Faulkner would rather have been Minister of Commerce, but Chichester-Clark successfully persuaded him that he was the right man to push through the various local government reforms. The post of Leader of the Commons and Chief Whip he gave to John Dobson, who had voted for Faulkner in the election stakes. He was also made a Minister of State. But the two appointments which raised the most eyebrows, were those of John Taylor and John Brooke. Taylor, the 32 year old MP for South Tyrone, was offered the post of Minister of State to Robert Porter, the Minister of Home Affairs. Brooke, the son of the former Prime Minister, Lord Brookeborough, was made a Minister of State to Roy Bradford, the Minister of Commerce and, in effect, became the Minister of Tourism. In making these last two appointments, Chichester-Clark was clearly taking a risk, but one he felt would offer an olive branch to those who had not given him their support in recent times and who had voted against him in the race for the premiership.

The remaining Ministers appointed were those who had served O'Neill. J. L. O. Andrews, the son of the second Prime Minister, John Andrews, remained leader of the Senate and Deputy Prime Minister. Finance stayed with H. W. Kirk and Robert Porter remained at Home Affairs. W. K. Fitzsimmons and R. H. Bradford continued at Health and Social Services and Commerce respectively. The only changes in ministry came for P. R. H. O'Neill, who moved to Agriculture, and Captain W. J. Long who moved to Education. In forming his first Cabinet, Chichester-Clark had, on the face of it, succeeded in effecting a fair balance of right and left wing Ministers. Those who assumed that he would simply appoint O'Neill's men were to be disappointed and those who considered that he would have a wholesale clearout were equally to be wrong footed. The *News Letter* intoned thus; 'Without making sweeping changes he [Chichester-Clark] has broadened the base of his new administration by bringing four leading critics of the old administration into his Government team'.[7] His first important and delicate task had been completed. Now he had to get on with the business of governing.

---

[7] *News Letter,* 5 May 1969

Building up confidences and facing realities

As an experiment at his first Cabinet meeting on 5 May 1969, the new Prime Minister decided to introduce informal meetings of his Ministers each Tuesday at noon. It seemed a wise and forthright step to take as he was clearly keen to ensure that the various ideas and proposals of all Ministers could and should be shared regularly with each other. This would, he considered, prevent friction amongst his senior team. For such a seemingly mild and unassuming man, Chichester-Clark took another bold and imaginative step. He announced an amnesty in over 130 cases for offences which had occurred from 5 October 1968 until 5 May 1969. Many were in prison for a wide ranging variety of felonies from serious crime to other shorter terms of imprisonment. Amongst those released were Ian Paisley and Major Ronald Bunting and charges were dropped against Gerry Fitt, Ivan Cooper, Paddy Devlin and Austin Currie and many others. The *Protestant Telegraph* seemed pleased; 'The unprecedented amnesty offered by Ulster's new Prime Minister has been enthusiastically welcomed by loyalist leaders. Major Chichester-Clark is most anxious to eradicate from Ulster all the distasteful traces of O'Neillism. The release of Dr Paisley and Major Bunting has demonstrated the new administration's desire to be firm and fair; and that is fairness without appeasement and firmness without oppression'.[8] In general there was widespread support for Chichester-Clark's actions and, for a little time – perhaps two months – he could enjoy a short honeymoon period. Even Paisley said he would give the new Prime Minister every opportunity to prove himself. The Prime Minister seemed pleased with what he had achieved in the first few days of his tenure in office.

On entering Stormont on 7 May for the first time as Prime Minister, Chichester-Clark followed parliamentary protocol and paid fulsome tribute to his predecessor, summing up his remarks by saying that 'He [O'Neill] always had a tremendous sense of duty'.[9] He went on to make a forceful and hard hitting speech. For himself, he declared that 'I will do my best' and continued by saying that 'this will be a government which favours no one, and which will offer justice to all'.[10] His upbeat speech impressed both friend and foe alike. He had made an auspicious start. Then, rather unusually

---

[8] *Protestant Telegraph*, 17 May 1969
[9] *Hansard col. 75*, 7 May 1969
[10] *News Letter*, 8 May 1969

some might say, he went off on an unexpected tangent just two days later. In a letter to the Moderator of the Free Presbyterian Church – the Reverend Ian Paisley – and in reply to his letter of the previous day, Chichester-Clark gave reassurances that care would be taken when meeting Taoisigh in future and that the inviolability of Northern Ireland and its borders was sacrosanct. 'Paisley pledged his support for the new Prime Minister provided he did not stray from traditional Unionism'.[11] Thus was the reason that Paisley would not, for the time being at any rate, cause too much discomfort to Chichester-Clark. Some would say that this was a wise step to muzzle the truculent demagogue, whilst others would doubtless consider it untimely and naïve. But Chichester-Clark was producing many elements of surprise, showing a degree of previously unseen wisdom and shrewdness.

He was soon out in the country speaking to various associations. Whilst in Fermanagh, he told local unionists that if nationalists stood by the democratic process he could see no difficulty in implementing the 'one man, one vote' legislation as soon as possible. The newspaper headline ran: 'Prime Minister does not fear "Green" Councils'.[12] In fact he had said that he would welcome forward looking steps from nationalist councils. This was a brave course of action for a fledgling Prime Minister to take, especially talking to nervous border unionists in this way; but it did also show the confidence which he exuded in those early days. He was commended and praised for speaking out against the vociferous minority in the columns of the newspaper of the unionist party; 'There can be nothing but admiration for this crisp air of action which Major Chichester-Clark has brought to his office and to the leadership of the Party'.[13]

In Stormont, Opposition members supported and welcomed the government's proposed new citizens' Complaints Bill which was to complement the power of the Ombudsman. The euphoria surrounding the Opposition's new found interest in Stormont was further enhanced on 20 May. The Prime Minister and three of his senior colleagues met all the Opposition MPs at Stormont for discussion on the government's programme and on the Opposition's requests for parliamentary time for

---

[11] Ed Moloney & Andy Pollak, *Paisley* (Swords 1986) p.179

[12] *News Letter*, 13 May 1969

[13] *Unionist*, May 1969

debates of their own instigation. This unprecedented meeting was described by both sides as 'cordial and friendly'.[14]

The heat is turned up a notch

But lurking in the background to prick the bubble of optimism was the Civil Rights Association (CRA). At the outset of Chichester-Clark's term it seemed to him that the CRA would be prepared to give him some respite. However, they had other ideas. With the bit now firmly between their teeth, they boldly announced that they would give the government just six weeks to issue a timetable for reform. There was to be no truce. Chichester-Clark, already making firm preparations with his Ministers to introduce reforms, was in no mood to assuage the Civil Rights Association. Reminding them that he was doing much to ensure that new legislation was well on course, he curtly rejected their ultimatum. He was determined not to have others set the pace. This may have worked at this juncture, but it was soon to fail. Setting the pace was all very well, but keeping ahead was going to prove a much more difficult exercise.

Another Prime Minister beckons

The first of Chichester-Clark's visits to 10 Downing Street took place on 21 May 1969. This was an early opportunity for the Northern Ireland Prime Minister to meet with his London counterpart, but it was not quite like a foreign or Commonwealth Prime Minister visiting London. This was a visit by an Ulster Prime Minister – a part of the United Kingdom which had, until recently, received but scant attention from Westminster. The Province's business, at that time, was dealt with along with Channel Islands and Isle of Man matters, together with the weighty concerns of vivisection and London taxi cabs. Affairs of the Northern Ireland state were of minor importance and left in the hands of a lowly Assistant Secretary. However Harold Wilson, now over five years as British Prime Minister, was beginning to realise that the trouble in Northern Ireland needed some of his attention. He had, of course, recently met Terence O'Neill to impress upon him the need for speedy reform following the riots in Londonderry and elsewhere. Now he was anxious to meet his successor, Major

---

[14] *News Letter*, 21 May 1969

Chichester-Clark. Two days before the visit by the Northern Ireland government team, the *News Letter* had indicated that 'Mr Harold Wilson has been impressed by the steps which have been taken by Ulster premier, Major James Chichester-Clark and his new administration towards remedying social and political grievances in Northern Ireland'.[15]

Chichester-Clark, accompanied by Commerce Minister, Brian Faulkner, and Home Affairs Minister, Robert Porter, spent over one and a half hours at 10 Downing Street with Wilson, James Callaghan the Home Secretary, and Lord Stonham, a Minister of State at the Home Office. They had useful discussions ranging from an update on the reform programme to the continuing need for additional funding for Northern Ireland industry. The general economic situation in the Province was also touched upon. Both sides agreed that the talks had been useful. The only negative side, however, was the discovery that, earlier the same morning, Bernadette Devlin, the newly elected MP for Mid Ulster, had called at Downing Street to hand in a letter from the Northern Ireland Civil Rights Association reiterating their civil rights demands. That call had surely been made to spike the Northern Ireland Prime Minister's guns. Nonetheless, Chichester-Clark and his Cabinet colleagues had every hope that much benefit would come from the meeting. In later days, however, they would become disappointed at the way in which Wilson would treat Northern Ireland and its citizens. James Chichester-Clark's dislike of Harold Wilson was taking firm root.

Their return to Stormont was greeted with acclamation. The lion had been bearded in his den and Chichester-Clark felt he had made good progress.

The honeymoon is short

Chichester-Clark had two visitors in his room on 22 May. The Reverend Ian Paisley and Major Ronald Bunting had been given an audience with the Prime Minister. Both these men had been released from the Crumlin Road Jail following Chichester-Clark's amnesty, but Bunting now had a difficulty. He had been deprived of membership of Down County Council and wanted to return. Not getting any satisfaction from the Council, he had decided to come straight to the top for redress and to demand

---

[15] *News Letter*, 19 May 1969

reinstatement from Chichester-Clark. The Prime Minister 'undertook to consider the representation'.[16] Support for the premier was still forthcoming from these men, a position not destined to persist for long. At around the same time, Chichester-Clark was required to declare that the 'B' Specials would stay, as they were needed to assist in civil disorder. Although he continued to plead for peace and goodwill, Chichester-Clark could begin to see the threads of contentment of his early days starting to unravel. The Civil Rights people were beginning to march once more and, on 2 June, they had a 'sit in' at Armagh City Hall. Trouble was brewing yet again.

In the early days of June 1969, Chichester-Clark made a visit to the Ulster office in London to attend a press briefing. It was favourably commented upon that he had taken the bother to travel to the capital just to spend a relatively short time meeting with the press. Positive comment boosted his self-esteem, something which was to suffer badly as the days went on.

Back in Belfast, however, the reality of being a Prime Minister already under fire was taking effect. In Stormont, Opposition MPs Paddy Devlin and James O'Reilly, were attacking Chichester-Clark for what they saw as the Prime Minister's half-hearted approach to peace and reconciliation in a troubled society. Chichester-Clark vehemently objected to their stance, declaring that he was fully committed to bringing about an early peaceful solution to the Province's present difficulties.

Faulkner was moving very quickly in preparing legislation for the setting up of the new central housing authority and reforming local government. Over the next number of months he was to face continued pressure, not only from the Civil Rights activists who were constantly demanding the reforms, but also from extreme unionists who were opposing these reforms. He was often to find himself between a rock and a hard place. But he pushed on with the zeal which marked him out as an enthusiastic politician who was determined to see the fruits of his labours fulfilled. As the weeks slipped by, a grudging admiration for his reforming work was expressed by a number of Opposition politicians. Faulkner himself, although still smarting from his defeat in the prime ministerial race, paid tribute to the Prime Minister. 'I found Chichester-Clark a loyal and helpful colleague with whom to work; he was honest and direct and I gained a new respect for him during the period that he was carrying the

---

[16] *News Letter,* 23 May 1969

burden of the premiership'.[17] The Civil Rights organisers, however, were not so accommodating and continued to pursue their demands with vigour.

In an upbeat speech on 3 June 1969, entitled 'Ulster on the move', the Prime Minister reminded his audience of the achievements of the Northern Ireland government, such as the setting up of a new university, the massive improvements at Harland and Wolff and the building of Ireland's first two motorways. He also wanted to squash the misapprehensions about the need to increase the franchise in local government elections. He declared 'Ours is no repressive and reactionary regime, but a Government clearly committed on its record to progress and reform. We will press ahead with our programme come what may; but our task will be made easier if we can do so with the sympathetic understanding of the people of Great Britain and of our friends further afield'.[18]

But Chichester-Clark realised that it was not only his Development Minister who was having his work cut out for him. Robert Porter, at Home Affairs, had to contend with what turned out to be the most intractable problems – the matter of Orange Order marches and of all other conflicting demonstrations. Almost daily, from June onwards, he had to consider applications for one parade after another. He needed to judge how the police would be able to control the crowds which would put a great deal of pressure on their meagre resources and inadequate forces. Initially, he was able to keep on top of the problem.

On 8 June, an Orange parade was scheduled to pass through the mainly nationalist town of Dungiven. Set at the entrance to the Glenshane Pass in County Londonderry, Dungiven was an obvious flashpoint for such a parade. Porter had given approval for the parade however, and the RUC prepared to keep the opposing factions apart. There were many ugly scenes and much wanton destruction in the town, but, in the end, the police were just about able to cope with this potentially critical situation. Even in these early days of what was to turn out very much as a summer of discontent, it was clear for all to see that the police were going to have trouble with these parades throughout the marching season. Other parades were banned or marches re-routed. Some went ahead 'on a wing and a prayer'. The police were under constant strain. There were just over 3,000 full time men in the

---

[17] Brian Faulker, *Memoirs of a Statesman* (London 1978) p. 56
[18] *Goverment of North Ireland Press Release*, 3 June 1969

force, with help from the Ulster Special Constabulary, the 'B' Specials. This latter force was not permitted to involve itself in matters of crowd control, but they were able to relieve their full time colleagues by guarding vital establishments and undertaking road checks.

A television appearance

After just ten weeks in power, Chichester-Clark decided that it was already time to present a 'state of the nation' speech on television. He knew that he was not a 'natural' on this medium, but he felt the situation now warranted such a performance. He reminded the people of the progress which his government was making and the fact that it was not helped by the sort of mindless violence recently perpetrated in Dungiven. He also 'lashed the Press…for putting Northern Ireland under the spotlight of publicity'[19] – the sort of adverse publicity which he considered unhelpful. His delivery was somewhat stilted, but his message was clear. To prove his point, the Prime Minister met with Opposition MPs again to ensure that they realised that his was an 'accessible administration'.[20]

There was a poignant interlude when the death of Earl Alexander of Tunis was announced on 16 June. (Chichester-Clark had worked closely with him as an ADC in Canada from 1947 until 1949). Services to commemorate this great soldier and statesman took place throughout the length and breadth of the United Kingdom and it was to St Anne's Cathedral in Belfast that those Ulstermen and women who had known Alexander repaired on Tuesday 8 July. Lady Alexander and her children, including the new Earl, were in attendance and were graciously welcomed to the Cathedral by the Dean, the Very Reverend Cuthbert Peacocke. The address was given by the Bishop of Clogher, Dr Alan Buchanan, and the lesson was read by James Chichester-Clark. Another link with the Prime Minister's past had broken, but he felt deeply honoured that he had been accorded such a prominent place in the obsequies of that great Ulsterman, Harold Alexander.

But, by the end of June, the six weeks' grace declared by the Civil Rights Association was ended and they now threatened to pump up the heat on Chichester-Clark. He responded by reminding them that such a

---

[19] *News Letter*, 12 June 1969
[20] *Ibid.*, 18 June 1969

return to street politics would 'kill stone dead'[21] any chance of attracting more industry. On 30 June he visited the Bogside where he met many of the hard pressed residents. This visit was appreciated if not entirely expected.

The first Ombudsman, Sir Edmund Compton, and the first Minister of Community Relations, Dr Robert Simpson, were by now appointed proving, if such were needed, that the reforms of recent times were now being put into practice. To Chichester-Clark and his colleagues such tangible progress exemplified their good intentions. How certain the population at large saw the move might well be another matter.

By the beginning of July came the first political fallout of his term of office. Chichester-Clark had to firmly and publicly rebuke his Minister of State, John Taylor, for making a speech which openly challenged the government's reform of local government franchise. Taylor had said at Downpatrick that such a proposal could lose unionists control of some councils to the nationalists and it was, therefore, obvious that he did not support this forward move of the government. Had Chichester-Clark made the correct decision to appoint such a maverick politician? He certainly would have to keep an even closer eye on his young Minister.

As the month of July brought its major parades, especially around the 12 July Orange Order demonstrations, so had Robert Porter to make more difficult decisions. He could hardly cancel these traditional marches but he knew that the possibility of confrontation was a real threat. Ian Paisley once again went to see the Prime Minister on 10 July to discuss marches and demonstrations.

For a period of three days, starting on 12 July, serious violence erupted in Londonderry and in other towns, causing Chichester-Clark to break off his holiday to convene an emergency Cabinet meeting. Porter, ominously, had called up the 'B' Specials to assist the over pressed full time RUC members. The 'B's were equipped with batons for crowd control – in a few short weeks they would be more heavily armed. The Minister also banned Civil Rights marches at this time. He had taken advice from the Inspector General of the RUC and felt he had no alternative but to take this action. Discontent grew amongst the nationalist community and, although the more realistic amongst them could see that the government was making some efforts on reform, the more extreme elements were contemplating other, less constitutional, means of promoting their cause.

---

[21] *News Letter,* 24 June 1969

And some Westminster MPs were predicting further civil disruption. 'Labour MP, Mr Stan Orme declared last night that the Chichester-Clark government was not strong enough to deal with new violence which may erupt soon in Northern Ireland'.[22]

Those inside and outside Northern Ireland felt a sense of foreboding. But there were glimmers of hope. On 6 August, a newspaper poll showed that 90% of the population of the Province wanted peace to be given a chance and that they 'would be glad to see an end to all parades and demonstrations for many months – and preferably a year'.[23] Would the rest of the summer months pass off peacefully without further trouble? In the end it was not to be.

[22] *News Letter*, 30 July 1969
[23] *Ibid.*, 6 August 1969

9

The Difficult Days of 1969

On 3 August Chichester-Clark summoned a special Cabinet meeting. It was to be the first of sixteen Cabinet meetings during that month alone. These senior politicians realised that, if the situation did not radically improve, there would be no alternative but to request troops to assist the civil power. Very serious rioting had broken out the previous day in the Shankill and Crumlin Road areas of Belfast. Catholic and Protestant rioters had attacked each other in the politically sensitive area of Unity Flats and the police had been seen as protectors of the Protestants and ambushers of the Catholics. Many Catholic homes were burnt out and the first of many evacuations from a mixed area to a religiously polarised area had commenced. The General Officer Commanding, General Freeland, wanted to make more use of the 'B' Specials before committing troops, but Chichester-Clark and Porter knew the dangers of such a move. The Cabinet wanted to press the British government for an early deployment of troops but, in the meantime, they demanded the use by the police of CS gas, which Porter diplomatically called 'tear smoke'.

On 8 August, Chichester-Clark and Porter went to see Callaghan in London. There was an angry confrontation between the Ulster premier and the Home Secretary when the topic of troops was discussed. Although no impasse was reached, the decision to deploy troops immediately was not taken at that meeting. Chichester-Clark determined to do the best he could with the forces available, such was the gritty calibre of the man. During the Downing Street talks it had been suggested to him that 'it would be advisable to endure a quite considerable degree of disorder before involving military assistance'.[1] The Cabinet members who had not been in

---

[1] *Northern Ireland Goverment Cabinet Papers,* 14 August 1969

London were appalled to hear the attitude of the British government of Harold Wilson. Direct rule had been considered causing both the Northern Ireland Prime Minister and his Cabinet secretary, Sir Harold Black, to express 'astonishment that such penal consequences could be in contemplation'.[2] They deeply resented the threats of the Home Secretary, James Callaghan, of a possible suspension of the Northern Ireland government in the event of troops being employed on a continuing basis in a peace-keeping role. This veiled intimidation raised the temperature within the Cabinet, and its members had to ensure that absolute secrecy was kept. Such a revelation could easily have led to a backlash which might have proved impossible to contain.

The Apprentice Boys of Derry were scheduled to have their annual march commemorating the relief of Derry in 1689, on 12 August. Such a parade in Londonderry would obviously be a test of the government's resolve to keep the peace and the Prime Minister had tried to persuade the organisers of the march to ban it voluntarily due to the prospect of serious trouble. The plea fell on deaf ears and, although the government could have prohibited the parade, the ban would have been ignored. Bus and trainloads of Apprentice Boys started arriving in the city early that day. The police had taken as many precautions as they felt they could, but were unsure as to whether or not they could prevent possible confrontations turning into riots. Chaos ensued.

In the staunchly nationalist Bogside area of the city, the nationalist population laid in wait for the marchers to pass by. They were prepared for a fight. Barricades had been pulled across the streets and, on top of the high-rise Rossville Flats, small boys ferried petrol up and down the stairs to youths who were making petrol bombs to throw at the police and marchers. And so the battle commenced. As soon as the marchers came within range, they were attacked with stones and bottles. The RUC interfaced the two rival factions and tried their best to keep them apart. They invaded the Bogside, only to be driven back by determined opposition. It was clear from the start that they were losing control of their objective and a group of well prepared vigilantes of the Derry Citizens' Defence Association soon took control of their area. For hours – in fact for more than 48 hours – hostilities raged. Many of the protagonists were injured and were taken off to have their wounds attended to. The serious disorder spilled over into the city itself and rioters started to fire many of

---

[2] *Northern Ireland Goverment Cabinet Papers,* 14 August 1969

the business premises in the city centre. Damage to life and property was considerable. The police, undermanned and over-stretched, were exhausted. They had been on duty for up to 16 hours each day and many had been injured in the affray. Many felt they could not carry on. At the end of the day, approval was sought, and received, from Robert Porter, the Minister of Home Affairs, for the police to use tear gas to disperse the mobs. By late on 12 August virtually all of the available 'B' Specials had been called out and they performed a most commendable job, not only in supporting their full time colleagues, but also in urging restraint on the Protestant rioters. Whilst this certainly had some calming effects on the crowd's excesses, rioting and burning went on for days. Law and order had broken down in Londonderry and in many other places in Northern Ireland. By the end of the three day period, five people had been killed and many more severely injured.

Frantic telephone calls were being made between Londonderry and Belfast and the Home Affairs Minister informed Chichester-Clark that the RUC could not continue without the help of the military. The watershed had been reached and the time had come to take more drastic action.

Agreement to deploy troops to Londonderry was made and, by 5 p.m. on 14 August, detachments of the Prince of Wales Own Regiment were on the streets of the Bogside. Troops were soon in place in Belfast where violence abounded. Serious rioting and shooting again took place on the night of 14/15 August in the Shankill and Falls areas of the city. There were open hostilities in the Divis Flats where two people, one a young boy and the other an off duty British soldier, were killed following the surprise, and unexplained, introduction of armoured cars to the streets. Mayhem reigned with more homes being torched and people fleeing their homes to stay with friends and relatives. On 15 August, Chichester-Clark requested that further troops be deployed in Belfast. Callaghan and Wilson readily acceded and soon the soldiers were seen on the streets of Belfast. By the tenth day, over 6,000 troops had been deployed. A crisis of major proportion had taken root in a part of the United Kingdom.

A broadcast to the people

Although still not keen on television broadcasts, Chichester-Clark realised that he must speak to the law-abiding people of Northern Ireland. This he did following the outbreak of rioting in the Bogside on the evening of 13 August. He told his audience that, for most of them, this was a day of shame. Considerable damage was being caused to the reputation of the Province and that damage to property was vastly expensive. He reminded them that reforms were in course of preparation and would be on the statute book just as soon as full debate had been held. He commended the hard working police and said how ashamed he was to see them lying exhausted on the streets of Londonderry. He announced the immediate recall of Stormont. Anarchy would not be allowed to prevail, although he was prepared, in the circumstances, to offer a truce to the people of the Bogside. He appealed for peace and for all right thinking people to make their voices heard. Although the stunned population listened with heavy hearts, many realised that a point of no return had been reached. Had not the arrival of troops and the admission that the local forces of law and order had not been able to cope, spelt out the fact that Doomsday had arrived?

Crossing swords with the Taoiseach

The usually good natured and even-tempered Taoiseach, Jack Lynch, could not contain himself when he saw what was going on in Londonderry. Nor, more pointedly, could many of his trenchant supporters. The redoubtable Charles Haughey was furious at the actions of the Northern Ireland government occasioned, probably, by the fact that his parents had come from the County Derry town of Swatragh. Lynch felt something had to be done and so he brought troops up to the border and set up field hospitals to treat those who were fleeing south in the aftermath of the riots. On the same day that Chichester-Clark had broadcast to the people in Northern Ireland, Lynch had broadcast to the people of the Republic and spoken of the unwarranted action by security forces in the north. He said that 'the present situation cannot be allowed to continue…that Stormont was no longer in control…and that the RUC is no longer accepted as an impartial police force'.[3] He urged the United Nations to send a peace keeping force to Northern Ireland and raised once more the spectre of partition. Even his opponents could hardly believe their ears when they heard the usually tolerant Lynch speak in such forceful terms. The southerners sat up and

---

[3] *News Letter,* 14 August 1969

listened. Was partition once again, after so many years, going to appear on the political agenda?

But what the people of the Republic and, for that matter, the people of Northern Ireland, did not expect to hear was the potency of Chichester-Clark's public reply and protest at the 'inflammatory and ill-considered'[4] words used by Lynch. He had heard 'with indignation the remarks of Mr Lynch' which he suggested were 'a clumsy and intolerable intrusion'.[5] The suggestion of a peace keeping force was 'quite ludicrous'.[6] Chichester-Clark had thus adopted the high moral ground in demanding that Lynch keep his nose out of northern affairs and declared the southern government 'unfriendly and implacable'.[7] 'The authorities in Northern Ireland played their chosen role well, reaffirming Mr Lynch's anti-partitionist credentials by means of a pompous denunciation on the part of Major Chichester-Clark, who was not sorry to testify to *his* Ulster orthodoxy'.[8]

Lynch did not expect this reaction from his mild-mannered neighbour. Nor did he expect to hear the senior Conservative politician, Reginald Maudling, criticise his speech as 'an irresponsible performance'.[9] In the weeks that followed, Chichester-Clark did not let up and continued to make many speeches against Lynch and southern interference. The case for a United Nations peace keeping force for Northern Ireland was firmly snubbed by both the British government and by the UN Secretary General. As a consequence, Jack Lynch largely retracted what he had said and, in a speech in Tralee at the end of the following September, he softened his attitude and even made reference to Article 44 of the Republic's constitution, which had always infuriated the northern population. This was the article which set out the special position of the Catholic Church in the Republic. Lynch was now publicly stating that it was time for a referendum to be held to amend this Article, the one which greatly offended the Protestants, both in the north and in the south. 'Mr Lynch had admitted in Tralee that any policy of seeking unity through agreement

---

[4] *News Letter,* 13 August 1969

[5] *Ibid.*

[6] *Ibid.*

[7] *Ibid.*

[8] Owen Dudley Edwards, *The Sins of our Fathers* (Dublin 1970) p. 314

[9] *News Letter,* 14 August 1969

must be long-term'.[10] Thus, by refusing to let the Taoiseach 'off the hook', the northern premier gained valuable support within his own jurisdiction.

Parliament recalled

Whilst the first troops into the Bogside were being cheered, given cups of tea and generally welcomed, Stormont was being recalled in emergency session. Chichester-Clark and his Cabinet colleagues considered it vital to do this in order to update the MPs on the situation. With Opposition members in attendance, a lengthy and often heated debate ensued. The Prime Minister spoke forthrightly and with emotion when he said – 'The people of Ulster, weary of strife, yearning for peace, fearful for their future, await our answer'.[11] Later, however, he was to be greatly disenchanted and dismayed when seven members of the Opposition group decided to walk out of the House when the debate reached discussion on the security situation. They were led out by the Foyle MP, John Hume, whose parting rejoinder summed up the views of his colleagues. 'I regret to say that the sterility of this House was never more in evidence than it is today…but after listening to Mr Taylor's speech, which was a jackboot speech in the present crisis, I can only say this in reply; we are quite firm, we shall not be moved. My colleagues and I, Mr Speaker, will say goodbye'.[12] This left just two Opposition Labour members in the chamber. This boycott of such important proceedings caused indignation and outrage amongst the unionist members. Later that evening Chichester-Clark summoned a group of twenty prominent businessmen and churchmen to Stormont to form a peace committee in a further endeavour to bring a semblance of normality back to the Province.

As the days following the introduction of troops passed, more and more barricades appeared on the streets of Belfast, Londonderry and in many other towns in the Province. The army made great efforts to encourage the residents in these areas to bring them down. They did have some success and some enclaves returned to a degree of sanity. However riots continued, almost unabated, in Newry, Lurgan, Dungannon and other

---

[10] *Belfast Telegraph,* 24 September 1969
[11] *Hansard col. 2247,* 14 August 1969
[12] *Ibid., col. 2290*

centres of population and the existence of ugly barricades remained an ongoing problem for some time.

The Downing Street Declaration and a fatal misunderstanding

Chichester-Clark's government looked as if it was losing its battle to hold on to its responsibility for Northern Ireland's security. By 20 August, security control had passed to the military at the insistence of Westminster. The previous day, Chichester-Clark and Porter had been with the Prime Minister, Harold Wilson, at 10 Downing Street. In order to spike Wilson's guns, they had previously decided (and these decisions had been minuted) to suggest that, in terms of security, the RUC and the 'B' Specials should immediately be put under the control of the army. At the same time, the 'B' Specials should be phased out of riot control duties. Other crucial points were discussed before both Wilson and Chichester-Clark were to speak on television, following the announcement of what became known as the Downing Street Declaration. This seven-point declaration had been agreed between both sides but Wilson, whether deliberately or not, was soon to 'put his proverbial foot in it'. Speaking first, whilst Chichester-Clark was being made up in a back room prior to his appearance, Wilson said that the 'B' Specials were to be phased out, without reference to the fact that the agreement had indicated that they would just be phased out of riot control duties. This caused a sensation in Northern Ireland – horror to the Protestants and disbelief to the Catholics.

When it was Chichester-Clark's turn to speak on television, *he had not heard what Wilson said and had no time to be briefed.* It therefore looked that he, as Ulster premier, had agreed to the total phasing out of the 'B's *which was never the case.* In subsequent discussions, Chichester-Clark clearly saw an ulterior motive in what Wilson had said. He had been seriously let down by the British Prime Minister when, to put it mildly, he least needed such a deliberate misunderstanding. On his return to Stormont, Chichester-Clark had a great deal of explaining to do to his MPs and others. In the end he was able to convince them all of Wilson's treachery whilst, at the same time, commending the remainder of the Declaration. He insisted on full support for these arrangements and that all unionist MPs fall in behind him, even those who had rarely supported him, especially in recent days. There were still others who felt that Chichester-Clark had not fought hard enough to retain more control. In looking back on that Wilson faux pas

Right: ADC Captain James Chichester-Clark, with Earl Alexander (left) and Air Marshal Guthrie (right) fishing on a wild Canadian river, summer 1948 (*Family collection*)

Below: Lord and Lady Alexander with their staff of Government House, Ottawa, with Captain Chichester-Clark (back row, extreme left) December 1947 (*Family collection*)

Below right: James Chichester-Clark, wearing bearskin, recruiting for the Irish Guards, in Banbridge, County Down, 1953 (*Family collection*)

Below left: Major Chichester-Clark, seated middle front row, with Irish Guards shooting squad, Germany, 17 March 1951 (*Family collection*)

Top left: James Chichester-Clark, as Minister of Agriculture, introducing Queen Elizabeth, the Queen Mother, to colleagues in Belfast, 1968 (*Tella Photography, London*)

Top right: James Chichester-Clark at his desk at Stormont in his early days as Prime Minister, June 1969 (*Manchester Daily Mail*)

Above: Minister of Agriculture, James Chichester-Clark, walking in the newly opened Gortin Forest Park, County Tyrone, with Prime Minister, Terence O'Neill, 9 June 1967 (*Family Collection*)

Left: Newly appointed Prime Minister, James Chichester-Clark, with his wife, Moyra, and his daughters Fiona (aged 8, right) and Tara (aged 6, left) at Moyola Park, May 1969 (*Century Newspapers*)

years later, Chichester-Clark acknowledged that he had been a fool for not insisting on seeing the text of what the British Prime Minister had said in his broadcast before he himself was interviewed. As ever, hindsight had been of little comfort to him. There was also, needless to say, strong and vociferous protest from outwith the chamber from Ian Paisley and others. He had only recently met with Chichester-Clark to suggest the setting up of a People's Militia' – an idea to which the Prime Minister had given some tentative support.

Chichester-Clark was continuing to show concern, not only about the breakdown of law and order, but also the fact that peace lines – the euphemism for ugly fences and barriers between communities – were more and more in evidence. He visited some of these areas and declared that he was confident that these measures could only be a temporary expedient. Little did he know that some of these so-called peace lines would still be in place 30 years later. However the very fact that he had taken time to go out into the streets to see what was going on for himself, earned James Chichester-Clark more than grudging admiration. For a time, the Prime Minister was a popular man.

The setting up of the Hunt Committee and the Scarman Tribunal

Chichester-Clark and Wilson had agreed that there should be a prompt report produced into the future of policing in Northern Ireland. Wilson announced that Lord Hunt, the conqueror of Everest, should be the chairman and that he and his committee would report very quickly to both governments. The committee was formally set up by Robert Porter, Minister of Home Affairs, on 26 August 1969. News of this impending report was not received with any enthusiasm in the Province, but Chichester-Clark was quickly able to convince any doubters in his own party of its efficacy. Before the end of August, the other two members of the Hunt enquiry team were announced. These were to be Mr Robert Mark, a future Commissioner of the Metropolitan Police in London, and Sir James Robertson, the Chief of Police in Glasgow. Their remit was 'to examine the recruitment, organisation, structure and composition of the Royal Ulster Constabulary and the Ulster Special Constabulary and their respective functions and to recommend as necessary what changes are required to provide for the efficient enforcement of law and order in Northern

Ireland'.[13] They were to set about their task quickly and, having met relevant interested parties and visited many police establishments, they were to have their findings ready by the end of September. With such a short time to present their report, the committee fell into the trap of meeting only with compliant groups and individuals. Those people who may have been able to shed more light on what was really needed to make acceptable changes in the police force were consequently not interviewed. When the report was published, the reaction, mainly of the majority, was entirely predictable – and negative.

At about this same time, the Scarman Tribunal was set up under Lord Justice Sir Leslie Scarman, assisted by Mr G. K. G. Lavery and Mr William Marshall, to investigate the troubles which had occurred between April and August 1969. With the Cameron Commission also due to report very soon on the troubles from October 1968 until April 1969, all this unwanted public glare was concentrated on Chichester-Clark and his government. One committee investigating would have been difficult to bear, two would have been infinitely worse, but three became the final straw which was, in the long term, to break the Northern Ireland government's back. The timing of the setting up of these committees was nothing short of disastrous.

A visit from 'Form Teacher' Callaghan

On 27 August, with his 'headmaster' Harold Wilson on holiday in the Scillies and out of the way, 'form teacher' Jim Callaghan arrived in Belfast. He was a big man, as tall and imposing as James Chichester-Clark, and he liked to create a 'presence'. He liked to imagine that he was a country gentleman. He set about his visit to Northern Ireland with great gusto, making all sorts of elaborate arrangements to meet all the major players in the Ulster conflict. He somewhat left Chichester-Clark in his wake. He met the clergy, including the rather reticent William, Cardinal Conway. He had a 'set to' with Ian Paisley and appeared to win the battle of words. He visited the Bogside where he was almost swamped by the crowds. He had to retreat to the house of one of the residents, to have tea and then to make an impromptu speech from an upstairs window. This is a picture which remains with Northern Ireland people to this day. He met the Cabinet on

---

[13] *The Hunt Report* (Belfast 1969)

two occasions and imposed his presence upon them. He spoke more than he listened and ensured that his message of speedy reform and the equalisation of the rights of the minority was plainly understood. He made it clear who in charge. Over his three days' visit, Callaghan certainly made an impression of a British Minister exuding confidence. 'He gave an air of a major-league performer showing the parish-pump locals how to run their affairs'.[14] In the end Callaghan had steadied the ship and, although he put Chichester-Clark and his Ministers in the 'tuppenny place', there was no British Minister Chichester-Clark liked more. On at least one occasion, he proved to be the life and soul of the party at Moyola Park hosted by the Prime Minister's wife.

Will this summer never end?

When Callaghan returned to London, he advised Chichester-Clark that he would be visiting again in October to see how the reform programme was progressing. Then Oliver Wright arrived in Belfast. His was not exactly a welcome arrival for, as the senior Whitehall civil servant with a mandate to 'work alongside the Northern Ireland Prime Minister and government', he was soon regarded with suspicion by unionist and nationalist politicians and local civil servants alike.

Barricades were becoming the bane of everyone's lives. They continued to rise like unsightly carbuncles throughout the towns and cities of the Province. The army, police and local representatives were doing their level best to have the barriers taken away and they continued to meet with some success. The Prime Minister, yet again, resorted to a television broadcast to appeal to the better nature of the citizens to pull down the barricades. He actually insisted on their removal and let the population know that the Province could make no progress with such visible evidence of sectarian strife in place. He had some limited success but it would be some further time before the streets were eventually cleared of all these obstacles.

On 12 September, the Cameron Commission report was published and copies eagerly purchased. By way of preparing the people for what the report contained, the Northern Ireland government published, as a preamble, a 'commentary' which set out what preparations they were

---

[14] Kenneth O. Morgan, *Callaghan – a Life* (Oxford 1997) p. 349

making for reform. For example, the Ombudsman had been appointed, the Hunt Committee was working on police reforms and the Scarman Tribunal was talking to witnesses. The main conclusions of Cameron were that there existed discrimination in housing allocation; there was gerrymandering of local authority boundaries; the 'B' Specials were a biased force; many of the Special Powers provisions were unacceptable; William Craig, as Home Affairs Minister, ought not to have banned the parade in Londonderry on 5 October 1968; there was evidence of subversive elements within the Civil Rights Association and there was clear ineptitude and even an element of brutality in the actions of the RUC. They made a number of recommendations to improve the security situation in Northern Ireland. There were many who thought that the recommendations were right and proper and others who took issue with them. But, in effect, there was so much else going on that Cameron was soon 'put on the back burner'.

In London, Callaghan was busy meeting with the self styled 'Peace Committee' from Belfast which consisted of twenty Catholics intent on ensuring that the British Home Secretary knew of their demands. Included in the group were Belfast MPs Gerry Fitt and Paddy Kennedy and the Catholic Bishop of Down and Connor, Dr William Philbin. Their meeting lasted over seven hours. Following this meeting, General Freeland was able to arrange for many more barricades to be dismantled.

At the same time, in Belfast at Ulster Unionist headquarters, Chichester-Clark was receiving a strong vote of confidence from party officials. He was in a more confident mood compared with his more despairing outlook of recent days.

Once again, however, any euphoria was short lived. After more trouble and unease in Belfast and Londonderry on 26 September, Ian Paisley – knowing, as usual, how to stoke a fire – orchestrated a huge anti-Cameron rally of 6,000 banner waving supporters on the steps of Stormont. The crowd, now looking to William Craig as their hero, as well as Paisley as their continuing saviour, jostled the Prime Minister and other MPs as they entered parliament that day. Chichester-Clark, although unmoved by the crowds reactions, did, however, realise the import of this troublesome gathering when he uttered this truism; 'I think it would have been well if we had grasped this nettle some time ago'.[15]

On 3 October Chichester-Clark and his Cabinet were given a copy of the Hunt Report which was due for publication within a few days. The

---

[15] *News Letter,* 1 October 1969

very next weekend, realising that the Hunt recommendations would not be to their liking, east Belfast Protestant mobs took to the streets causing more destruction to property and difficulty for the police. To add to his sorrows, the Prime Minister learnt, with much regret, that the brilliant and moderate unionist MP for South Antrim, Richard Ferguson, was to resign his seat having 'been subjected to intimidation since he left the Orange Order in August'.[16] The greatest implication of this resignation, of course, was the insistence on Orange Order membership as a requisite for a unionist MP. To moderates like Ferguson, membership of the Order was clearly unnecessary but this view did not yet hold anything like universal sway. In fact Chichester-Clark, two months later, pointedly indicated that membership of the Orange Order was a 'private' matter.

Publication of the Hunt Report

As he promised – or threatened – he would, James Callaghan returned to Belfast for his second visit on 9 October. He was to find this visit an altogether different 'kettle of fish'. Things did not run so smoothly and, when he left on 13 October, he realised that he was not quite the darling of the Ulster crowds that he had been during his late August visit.

Rumours had started to circulate in police circles and amongst the public at large that Hunt would, amongst other things, be recommending the abolition of the 'B' Specials. Chichester-Clark remained very tight-lipped because, by now, he knew the contents of the report and that the 'B' Specials were to be disbanded.

The report became public on 10 October. It came 'as an appalling shock to Protestant opinion'.[17] It was sold out in a matter of a few hours. It became essential reading. There were 47 recommendations, many of them innocuous enough, but a number causing a not unexpected storm. The major proposals were as follows: the creation of a Police Authority to include a wide representation of the local population; the end of military style duties of the RUC; the disarming of the RUC; the setting up of a police reserve; a central recruiting system with a view to encouraging more Catholics to join the force; an increase in the force numbers; the changing of the colour of the uniform to blue and the abolition of the 'B' Specials to be

---

[16] *News Letter*, 8 October 1969
[17] Sunday Times Insight Team, *Ulster* (Harmondsworth 1972) p. 160

replaced by a part time force under army control. Chichester-Clark and his Cabinet clearly understood the implications of the report and Callaghan, now more and more breathing down their necks, was insisting on full and speedy implementation.

It was these last two recommendations which caused the greatest protests. The RUC members, to a man, refused to change the colour of their uniforms. But the issue of disbanding the 'B' Specials caused the greatest furore and created the biggest problem for the Prime Minister. He, himself, had always the greatest regard for the Ulster Special Constabulary, but, knowing by now that there was not going to be any alternative to the phasing out of the 'B' Specials, he was hardly in a position to protest. He also knew that the proposed Ulster Defence Regiment would, to all intents and purposes, replace the USC. He now issued a threat to his recalcitrant backbenchers that, if he were defeated on Hunt, he would call a general election. Following the acrimonious debates in the Commons, Chichester-Clark received the support he required, although seven of his unionist MPs, including William Craig and Harry West, voted against the measures with a further two MPs abstaining.

Out in the towns and villages, there was disbelief and despair that the Specials were to be disbanded. Almost inevitably, more serious rioting throughout the Province erupted. The Belfast *News Letter* headline on 13 October read, 'Guns out again on the Shankill Road'.[18] Militant mobs attacked the police they wanted to protect. The army responded by using considerable force and firing on the crowds, causing the deaths of two civilians. Tragically, during these exchanges, Constable Victor Arbuckle, was shot dead – the first RUC man to die in the 'Troubles'.

In the wake of this outbreak of violence, Chichester-Clark made another television appearance in which he again appealed for calm and restraint. As ever he found this a difficult ordeal but he felt that he had to tell the people what he thought and he needed them to know that support for the Hunt recommendations was essential for the future of Northern Ireland. Many, however, considered that Chichester-Clark was a traitor to them and large numbers of Specials resigned, with their associations passing votes of no confidence in the Prime Minister. As time went on, most 'B' Specials accepted the decision and recruitment for the replacement force – the Ulster Defence Regiment – soon commenced with many former 'B' Specials actually opting to join the new force. The uniforms for the RUC

---

[18] *News Letter,* 13 October 1969

were never changed to blue and the recommendation made by the Hunt Committee that the name of the force was not be changed was met with a sense of relief amongst the majority of the population. But, ominously, the Committee made this admission; 'As to the future, the IRA and the revolutionary socialists, using their position in the Civil Rights Association, seem likely to maintain civil rights pressure; and this will no doubt generate Protestant reaction'.[19] Here the committee acknowledged the active and prominent part played by the IRA in the marches to date, something the Northern Ireland government had been slow to appreciate. Had this pointer been earlier understood and acted upon, then the infiltration by the subversives into the CRA organisation could have been nipped in the bud.

However in the aftermath of the report's findings, the Inspector General, Mr Anthony Peacocke, suddenly retired. He was replaced by a favourite of James Callaghan's, Sir Arthur Young, formerly of the Metropolitan Police. Sir Arthur became the first Chief Constable of the RUC, but he was generally unpopular with politicians and RUC men alike and Chichester-Clark considered him 'a political liability'.[20] It seemed that neither Young nor the GOC, Sir Ian Freeland, had anything very complimentary to say about the local police. Sir Arthur Young only stayed in the Province for just over a year before returning to England, no doubt relieved to be rid of such a quirky force. For the time being Callaghan, somewhat chastened, was happy to be returning to London.

Vagaries of domestic politics

In a buoyant speech in his own constituency of South Londonderry on 17 October, Chichester-Clark issued a clarion call 'for Unionist unity and discipline'.[21] He was pleased to see that the RUC were starting to break down some of the wretched 'no-go' areas, such as those in the Bogside and the Falls, and he was imposing his will on the party by expelling recalcitrant members such as Craig and West. He felt firmly in command, and when he received a 5 to 1 endorsement of his leadership at a full meeting of the Ulster Unionist Council called to discuss the Hunt Report on

---

[19] *The Hunt Report*, paragraph 26

[20] Sunday Times Insight Team, *Ulster* (Harmondsworth 1972) p. 172

[21] *News Letter*, 18 October 1969

24 October, he positively exuded confidence once more. 'Afterwards Major Chichester-Clark said "I think we have come away from this meeting as a pretty united party"'.[22] Later in November, however, Chichester-Clark suffered the acute local embarrassment of being ousted as Vice-Chairman of the Castledawson branch of the Ulster Unionist Association. His successor was Mr Frank Taylor, a local bus driver. The local unionists said that there was nothing personal about the change in the local party committee, but it proved to be bad publicity for Chichester-Clark. He had held this post for many years and he must have realised that there was some significant discontent amongst rank and file unionists about the Hunt Report and its ramifications, particularly those concerning the 'B' Specials.

In November, too, Chichester-Clark made a major speech to the Larkfield unionists on the southern outskirts of Belfast. This was a constituency with a large Catholic electorate, yet the unionist, Basil McIvor, had been elected in February 1969 with a majority of over 6,000 votes, clearly showing that many Catholics had voted for him. At the meeting, the topic of Catholics becoming members of the unionist party came up. Chichester-Clark made it clear that Catholics were every bit as welcome to join the party as anyone else who was prepared to support the Northern Ireland constitution. He said that they could expect exactly the same privileges as any other member, and that ultimately they could aspire to any position. This was clearly a reference to their becoming party officials or even MPs. However circumstances dictated that it was well nigh impossible to be selected as a unionist candidate if a person was a Catholic. He was reminded of the infamous case of Louis Boyle who had sought the unionist nomination in South Down in the February general election, but who had been ultimately unsuccessful in his bid. There were, and always had been, a small number of Catholic members, but the situation changed as the Troubles continued. It now seemed unsafe to show allegiance to the unionist cause, no matter how pro-Union any Catholic was. Whether they liked it or not, liberal Catholics had to lie low lest their liberalism might be construed as support for a regime which the hard liners amongst them felt they now had 'by the throat'.

Further splits were now appearing in the party. John Taylor, the Minister of State, made a controversial speech early in November challenging membership of the Ulster Unionist Party by those who now belonged to the recently formed New Ulster Movement (NUM). In clear

---

[22] *News Letter,* 25 October 1969

and unequivocal terms, Taylor denounced those who sought to be members of both organisations. He clearly pointed out that NUM supporters could not be Ulster Unionists as well. The row went on for a long time and Chichester-Clark became more and more embroiled in the matter. The rules of the party were examined and, after much acrimonious debate, the Ulster Unionists decided that NUM members could not remain members of the Ulster Unionist Party. The publicity, however, did the Prime Minister no good at all and his unhappiness at Taylor's antics opened up unnecessary divisions within the increasingly troubled parliamentary party.

By now, too, the RUC was patrolling the streets unarmed for the first time since 1922. This was doubtless a very significant event, but the experiment was not to last for very long.

More discussions in London

Chichester-Clark travelled to London on 17 November to have further talks with Wilson and Callaghan. Although the chief reason for the meeting was to update the British Ministers on the present state of affairs in the Province, Chichester-Clark raised two issues causing him particular concern. By now recruitment for the Ulster Defence Regiment had started and, because this force was seen by many in the minority population as simply a replacement for the 'B' Specials, it was obvious that Catholics would resist joining the new regiment. Thus it retained a preponderance of Protestants in a force which had been intentionally set up to reflect the overall population in the Province. There was also the fear expressed by the Ulster premier that the outlawed Ulster Volunteer Force was again showing its ugly head. With soothing reassurances from Downing Street, Chichester-Clark returned, somewhat diffidently, to Belfast.

Nevertheless, the security situation back home was quieter. Events at Stormont were on a firmer footing and it looked as if the Opposition parties would come together. Chichester-Clark felt able to support a united opposition. 'The whole of Ulster was waiting for real leadership from the Opposition side and if that leadership can now be shown, we for our part will not seek in any way to perpetuate old differences'.[23] With Patrick McCrory now heading up a six man body to review the new proposals for

---

[23] *News Letter*, 12 December 1969

local government and with the festive season approaching, the Prime Minister felt that progress was being made – and being seen to be made – even though there was still a lot to achieve. However, as always, there were a couple of matters which were going to take the icing off the Christmas cake. The hue and cry over the 'no-go' areas would not die down and, just three days before Christmas, Bernadette Devlin, that darling of many of the so-called oppressed minority, was jailed for six months for her part in the August Bogside riots. It was going to be the case of making the best of what was going for him as James Chichester-Clark prepared for the festive season.

A split in the IRA

Following their last campaign in Northern Ireland from 1956 to 1962, the IRA had been quiescent. Thus, when the trouble came into the Catholic areas in Belfast in August 1969, some of the local population looked to the IRA to act as their protectors. They looked in vain for support and it was not long before graffiti appeared on city gable walls displaying the derogatory inscription 'IRA – I ran away'. Some of the remnant IRA members in Belfast realised what was happening and that, if they were to be in a position to help those who sought their assistance, they would need to take more decisive action. This was not the way headquarters in Dublin saw the situation. They aspired to a political way forward and they did not wish to see a return to the gun. This clearly did not impress some of the more militant Belfast members who then sought to break out of the IRA circle to engage in an armed struggle. After various meetings in the north and in Dublin, the split came. By the beginning of 1970, there emerged the Provisionals, or the 'Provos', whose main plank was to use force to rid the north of what they saw as the enemy – the government of Chichester-Clark, the existence of Stormont and the presence of the British army. With Billy McKee as their first Chief of Staff and with no more than perhaps 30 men, the 'Provos' entered the bloody fray. Chichester-Clark had sufficient intelligence to know much of what was happening. It created some discomfiture to him and his government to know that the IRA was, once again, a disruptive force to be dealt with just as 1970 had opened in relative calm.

10

Enemies Within and Without

The Special Powers Act had been a bone of contention for years. It was one of the strongest platforms from which the Civil Rights Association was lambasting the government. It was, perhaps to most of the population, an unnecessarily controversial piece of archaic legislation and it gave too many coercive powers to Stormont, powers which even Westminster did not possess. It even included provision 'to inflict whipping'. Consequently, part of the reform package included a close look at the Act's repressive enactments. The Attorney General, Basil Kelly, was given the job, with a committee to assist him, of reviewing the Act to make recommendations. After deliberating for more than four months, Kelly recommended that the Act be scrapped more or less in its entirety. During January, the subsequent Public Order Bill was debated in Stormont and the contributions of many MPs were vehement and vitriolic. Most members made their views strongly felt and there was much filibustering. Debates even lasted, on some occasions, through the night – something almost unheard of in the usually somnolent chamber. The Senate also deliberated long and hard over the Bill's clauses, with many of them being dissected word by word before a decision was reached. In the end, however, on 23 January 1970, the Bill was eventually passed into law, unaltered. The strain of dealing with this legislation put the Minister, Robert Porter, under unrelenting pressure and there were rumours abounding that he wanted to resign. He denied that this was the case and carried on in his defence of the new public order measures. But chinks in the armour of Chichester-Clark and his hard pressed Ministers were beginning to appear. Never in the history of the Northern Ireland parliament had there been such a raft of far reaching measures put through and opponents on both their own side and the Opposition continued to bring great weight to bear on the government.

During the weekend of 24/25 January 1970, serious rioting broke out yet again in the Protestant Shankill area of Belfast. Such was the severity of the outbreak that trouble lasted well into the following week. Support for the forces of law and order ebbed away when 'Paratroopers dealt harshly with Shankill rioters during four nights in January when they attempted to break through to Catholic streets'.[1] Although the RUC had tentatively returned to patrol the streets of the Catholic Falls area a few days before, this did not assuage the hard-line Protestants who had been calling for the return of law and order to all parts of the Province. Now they felt that their 'own forces' were venting their spleen on them – and they did not like it.

The usual port in another storm

With tension perceptibly rising again throughout the Province and with the calm of the first days of the New Year dissipating, Chichester-Clark hurried again to visit Callaghan in London. The Belfast morning newspapers anticipated the visit. 'Major Chichester-Clark discusses Ulster's future with the Home secretary in London today against a background of heightening tension in the Province'.[2] Knowing that the security situation was difficult and that unemployment was continuing to rise, he had to return to Belfast with more than just fine words from Callaghan. Chichester-Clark did come back later in the day with a substantial aid package aimed to please his own MPs as well as those of the Opposition.

Yet again the Prime Minister found out how difficult was the position he held. He was hardly back in his office at Stormont when rumours emerged of a threat to his leadership. By way of countering this unwelcome tittle-tattle, and just prior to the Queen's speech at Stormont, Chichester-Clark gave a full scale interview to the *News Letter*. In it he was optimistic once more and, in denying that his party was moving to the right, declared 'Now we look to a brighter future. The Government has shown the will to change: Parliament had provided the concrete evidence of change...We want to make Ulster a happy and prosperous place in which to live'.[3] Two days later – on his 47th birthday – he set off on a top

---

[1] Jonathan Bardon, *A History of Ulster* (Belfast 1992) p. 677

[2] *News Letter,* 4 February 1970

[3] *Ibid.,* 10 February 1970

secret flight to England where he spent part of the weekend briefing members of the press corps about his assurances of better times in store for Northern Ireland.

Serious opposition within party ranks

Chichester-Clark had good support from his senior Ministers and most of his backbenchers until well into 1970. Brian Faulkner was zealous in his pursuit of reforms and was showing the way forward. But, by the end of February, trouble was brewing within the party. The Police Act, as part of the legislation introduced after the recommendations of the Hunt Report, was passing through Stormont. It was creating problems for the Prime Minister and a number of dissident MPs were threatening to oppose the measures contained in the Act. Having to swallow the fact that the RUC was now unarmed and that there were not even to be weapons available in police stations, proved too much for five prominent members – West, Craig, McQuade, Laird and Mitchell. They determined to vote against the government. Chichester-Clark immediately countered by warning them that they would be expelled if they dared to vote against the government. The *News Letter* saw the dangers inherent for the Prime Minister. 'Major Chichester-Clark is facing the most serious threat to his premiership since he formed his administration a year ago'.[4] In an effort to diffuse the situation, Chichester-Clark summoned West and Craig to meet him. But rather than solve the difficulties, it only exacerbated them. The Prime Minister decided to table a 'confidence' vote in the Commons to show who was in charge. But his proposed action was seen as unhelpful by his own supporters in the parliamentary party – they felt that Chichester-Clark should have expelled the dissidents at once rather than prolonging the agony. When the vote eventually came in Stormont on 18 March after a short, trenchant speech from the Prime Minister, only the 'honest man' McQuade voted against the legislation, whilst the other four abstained. They were then peremptorily expelled from the parliamentary party. The split in the House dismayed many unionist MPs.

Some days previously, on 6 March, at yet another meeting of the Ulster Unionist Council, Chichester-Clark did receive a handsome vote of confidence from the assembled delegates. Yet he knew that, amongst other

---

[4] *News Letter*, 11 March 1970

problems, disunity in the party was manifesting itself in different guises. In west Ulster, mainly in Fermanagh, dissension was evident and this was 'known to be of concern to the Premier'.[5] In local associations in different parts of Northern Ireland, votes of 'no confidence' in the Prime Minister were being passed. There were even some MPs who were expressing the view that the Prime Minister 'could well be on his way out',[6] and, on the other side, members of the Civil Rights Association demonstrated against Chichester-Clark when he was giving a speech at a London hotel on 13 March.

On 22 March, Chichester-Clark attended a special gathering in the King's Hall in Belfast to commemorate 50 years of service given by the Ulster Special Constabulary. In an emotionally charged address to a very large group of people, which included many previous Inspectors General of the RUC and other dignitaries, the Prime Minister recalled, with much pride, the selfless service given by the 'B' Specials. They had endured many difficult years, particularly in the early days of Northern Ireland's existence and more so in the recent troubled times. The genuineness of his speech clearly showed his own personal admiration for a body of men whom many had now seen cause to vilify. The fact that the force was shortly to fade into oblivion had certainly hit a raw nerve in the normally placid and impassive premier.

Continuing problems and Easter disruption

'No-go' areas were beginning to proliferate; a steady increase in explosions was beginning to make its mark; vigilantes were beginning to flex their muscles. Chichester-Clark understood that if these problems were not removed, and removed soon, the emerging terrorist organisations would gain too firm a foothold. But he did not get enough support from the security chiefs or from Westminster. He hit out at what he considered to be 'ham-fisted and biased' remarks of Wilson made on 25 March. 'Anyone who supposes that the troubles of Northern Ireland are wholly attributable to the acts of the unionist party over the past 50 years shows an extraordinary lack of understanding of the true and very complex

---

[5] *News Letter,* 6 March 1970
[6] *Ibid.,* 12 March 1970

situation'.[7] These pointed remarks came just days before further disruption at Easter. There was serious rioting in Belfast and in the Bogside in Londonderry as well as trouble with parades in Armagh. The army had to resort to the use of CS gas which finally turned most Catholics against them. They felt that the army had been transformed into yet another tool of unionist oppression. They finally turned their backs on the forces of law and order to follow the dictates of the terrorists whose power was ever increasing.

When the new Ulster Defence Regiment came into being on 1 April – still with a disappointing number of Catholic recruits – they experienced a baptism of fire. With further fierce west Belfast riots, their assistance was quickly required and their determination tested. In a lengthy interview with Mervyn Pauley of the *News Letter* on 8 April, Chichester-Clark, in more reflective mood, stated that 'we have a duty to future generations. The silent majority must speak out'.[8]

Impending by-elections and further disaster

When Terence O'Neill had resigned from Stormont not long after his ennoblement (he could have remained as an MP at Stormont as a peer of the realm) Chichester-Clark and his cabinet colleagues did not need to be told how difficult the subsequent by-election campaign in Bannside would be. Ian Paisley, who had come so close to defeating O'Neill in February 1969, was sure to fight the seat. And it came as no surprise, therefore, when he filed his nomination papers. At the same time his colleague, the Reverend William Beattie, opted to fight the South Antrim vacancy caused by the resignation of Richard Ferguson a short time before. The government had a fight on its hands, knowing that defeat by the Protestant Unionists could spell disaster for the future of the reforms of Chichester-Clark. And so the heavyweights, like former premier Brookeborough and Chichester-Clark himself, were brought into the two constituencies in support of the Ulster Unionist candidates. The Prime Minister, realising the party's particularly precarious position in Bannside, felt he should make as great an effort there as possible in order, as he said, 'to support Terence's past'. He wanted to show his spirited determination, and that of his

---

[7] *Irish News*, 26 March 1970

[8] *News Letter*, 8 April 1970

administration, to ensure the election of the Ulster Unionist candidate, Dr Bolton Minford. Over the weeks preceding the poll a veritable dogfight took place, with Paisley using his vitriolic rhetoric to impose his views upon the people of the constituency's sleepy towns and villages such as Randalstown and Rasharkin, and throughout Bannside. The government speakers tried their level best to encourage the constituents to vote unionist but, in the end, their pleas were to no avail. Their opponents easily won the seats. 'Paisley and Beattie sweep into Stormont – a double rebuff for the Chichester-Clark administration'.[9]

These election defeats were a real blow to James Chichester-Clark. He could not disguise the fact that, try as he might to put a brave face on things, the forces of extremism were taking a firm hold on politics in Northern Ireland. To add further fuel to the fire, and to add to Paisley's triumphalism, came the advent of another political party. The 'middle of the road' Alliance Party, which aimed at attracting moderate Catholics and Protestants, was launched on 21 April 1970. It had been a bad month for Chichester-Clark – there was no disguising the fact. He could only hope that there might be something which could change his fortunes. The evening newspaper, at the end of his first year in power, rather sadly reflected that 'His year in office will be remembered as the time when we stopped being a state and became a shire'.[10]

He did have the satisfaction of a personal triumph when he received a standing ovation at a meeting of the Ulster Unionist Council on 25 April. However the truth of the matter was that his majority at that meeting was just 277 to 203 and some delegates seemed anything but enamoured of him.

Gun running in the Republic and a British general election

It would be true to say that some pressure was taken off the Northern Ireland Prime Minister when, on 6 May 1970, the Taoiseach, Jack Lynch, caused a sensation by sacking two of his Cabinet Ministers, Charles Haughey and Neil Blaney. This followed the receipt of a report from the Garda Siocanna that the names of these Ministers had been mentioned in connection with illegal importation of arms to the Republic. After the

---

[9] *News Letter,* 17 April 1970
[10] *Belfast Telegraph,* 30 April 1970

Bogside riots the previous August, a considerable amount of money had been donated to give assistance to those in Northern Ireland who were in distress. The Republic's government had tried to have this money distributed in the north by the Irish Red Cross, but permission to do so had been withheld by the British authorities. The allegation against Haughey and Blaney was that they had knowingly conspired to have this money 'laundered' in fictitious bank accounts to enable it to be used to purchase arms. There certainly were many suspicious events, including gun running into Dublin airport from Belgium. There were rumours that Lynch himself had some knowledge of these nefarious happenings and that a number of his Cabinet colleagues also knew what was going on. Lynch's hand was forced when the opposition Fine Gael leader, Liam Cosgrave, came into possession of more incriminating information. Only then did Lynch act, asking the Ministers for their resignations. Initially they refused to go, but after Lynch appealed to President de Valera, the men eventually did resign. They left office, in disgrace, in May. Their first court case, in September, was declared a mistrial and at their subsequent trial in October, the defendants were acquitted.

Chichester-Clark and Harold Wilson had followed the progress of these events with considerable interest, but were glad to see that Lynch had survived as Taoiseach and had not been toppled. Not only had he remained in office, but his popularity in the Republic had soared to an all-time high. The whole affair, however, had left a bad taste in the northern premier's mouth.

By the middle of May, it became clear that Harold Wilson was about to call a British general election. Although Chichester-Clark warned James Callaghan that an election at this time would 'cause fresh trouble in the Province',[11] the plea was ignored and 18 June was named as the date for the country, including, of course, a tense Northern Ireland, to go to the polls. Now the British government had definitely 'taken their eyes off the Northern Ireland ball'. The Labour administration's full attention had now to be concentrated on getting themselves re-elected. It would be a difficult task and whether or not the strain of the impending election had some adverse effect on Wilson, he certainly did make a number of faux pas at the beginning of June. He first blundered on 1 June when he informed his listeners that 'his government had to intervene after 50 years of Tory rule to

---

[11] *News Letter,* 14 May 1970

guarantee an orderly and a fair society in Northern Ireland'.[12] On 5 June he criticised the pace of Chichester-Clark's reforms – 'a lot has been done but far too late in the day'.[13] These remarks infuriated the Ulster premier but, as ever, he kept his peace. There was too much to do to ensure the return of Ulster Unionist MPs to Westminster and, with Ian Paisley determined to field candidates, including himself, the task was not going to be an easy one. Unusually for a Stormont premier, Chichester-Clark took a high profile in the campaign. He canvassed widely for his Westminster colleagues. A row of some dimension arose when he was assailed with the rumour that he had 'done a deal' with Paisley to prevent the unionist vote being split in constituencies where such a division would see an anti-unionist candidate elected. His own brother's constituency of Londonderry was mentioned as one where a splitting of the vote in unionism could defeat Robin Chichester-Clark, but this was something he vehemently denied. He was, after all, the first of the unionist MPs to speak out publicly against Paisley and his antics and he could never see what benefits such a deal could have accrued. James Chichester-Clark also denied that there had been any such 'arrangement', but, when Paisley himself at the end of the campaign said that there certainly was truth in the allegations, he found the situation somewhat uncomfortable. It seems likely that some, even very insignificant, deal had been done.

When election day dawned, the establishment was quite obviously concerned. The Ulster Unionists usually won at least 11 of the 12 seats but, when the votes were counted and declared, they only held 8 seats, their lowest number ever. The flamboyant electioneer Paisley had defeated the less colourful Henry Clarke in North Antrim and the Marquess of Hamilton, facing just a single nationalist opponent, lost to Frank McManus in Fermanagh/South Tyrone. Bernadette Devlin and Gerry Fitt had held their Mid Ulster and West Belfast seats with some ease. It had not been a good day for the Ulster Unionists and Chichester-Clark's warnings of disaster to Callaghan had been realised. And to make matters worse, the Labour Party lost their gamble and power transferred to Edward Heath and his Conservative party. Chichester-Clark, therefore, had some expectation that this new administration might be more helpful to the Northern Ireland problems, but this was to prove not to be the case.

---

[12] *News Letter*, 2 June 1970

[13] *Ibid.*, 5 June 1970

On the security front, trouble regularly arose when burnings, rioting and murder continued to terrorise the streets of the Province. During the month of May, various hauls of arms were found within both camps, causing considerable disquiet to Chichester-Clark and the security chiefs. At the end of June, after a period of relative calm, further violent riots broke out in Belfast and Londonderry and, after four full days of disruption, six people lay dead. The question on everyone's lips now was 'Will the 12th of July marches be allowed to go ahead?'

Another marching season: another government in London

Reginald Maudling, the new Conservative Home Secretary, visited Northern Ireland for the first time in his new capacity at the beginning of July. For him it was to be a baptism of fire. He had scarcely landed in the Province when he became engulfed by a controversy about the Special Powers Act. On the one hand, unionist backbenchers were demanding that the police and army were given clear and unequivocal instructions to shoot down snipers when they were identified and, on the other hand, Opposition MPs were expressing their utter revulsion at the rumour that internment was on the agenda. Combined with these political assaults from all sides, Maudling was appalled to witness the violence and destruction wrought on people and property by carefully planned terrorist attacks which occurred during the weekend when he was in Belfast. He listened to Chichester-Clark's condemnations of this orgy of fire raising and raw intimidation as he struggled to come to terms with the poisoned cup he had received from Edward Heath. It was not long before he fully understood how difficult a task it was to be in charge of security in Northern Ireland; neither was it long before he showed his frustration at his dilemma in ways not considered entirely appropriate for a politician of his calibre.

At the same time, Chichester-Clark and his government were pushing the Criminal Justice Bill through Stormont and this was proving to be a tricky task. For a full 19 hours the debate raged in the Commons. Paisley and Beattie were effectively challenging the legislation line by line. The main effect of this new law, passed and put on to the Statute books on 1 July 1970, was to introduce a mandatory six month prison sentence for what could previously have been described as relatively minor offences such as riotous behaviour. This clearly meant that rioters arrested during disturbances, which were occurring with frightening frequency, were being brought before resident magistrates who had no option but to imprison the offenders for six months if they were found guilty. The prisons were filling up, the magistrates were becoming exasperated and the Chief Constable, Sir Arthur Young, 'was appalled'[14] at what was happening. Magistrates and police alike were calling for the immediate repeal of this law. Although it was eventually removed from the Statute books in December, inter community strains continued to appear. The police did have some discretion in reducing the 'riotous behaviour' charge in some cases, but it seemed to the Catholic minority that the RUC was giving this leeway only to Protestants. This may or may not have been the case, but instead of the law improving the situation, its effect was entirely the opposite and minority support, which had been gradually coming over to the government side, soon dissipated. Instead of giving Chichester-Clark further kudos, this law weakened his position.

Many of the members of the RUC had been expressing their support for being unarmed, much to the surprise of the population. They felt that, by having the army there to support them, their position could now be seen as that of a more traditional police role. But there were many in the force who did not agree with this sentiment and, in the middle of the following September, a vote amongst the members of the force was taken which showed only a narrow majority in favour of remaining unarmed. The Prime Minister expressed his pleasure at this decision, although he clearly understood the reasons for the slim majority.

To march or not to march – that was the question

In the prevailing current of fear and disruption, it seemed to many that the wisest counsel to the government would be to advise that the traditional 12th of July parades should be called off, at least for 1970. The Chief Constable so advised; Maudling and the British government so commended; Chichester-Clark himself indicated that 'he would be greatly relieved if the Orange marches of July 13th* were called off'.[15] He appeared on television on 10 July to appeal for restraint. But, in the event, perhaps

---

[14] Sunday Times Insight Team, *Ulster* (Harmondsworth 1972) p. 226
* The 12th of July 1970 was a Sunday and these traditioinal parades are never held on Sundays.
[15] *News Letter,* 7 July 1970

wiser counsel prevailed. The GOC felt, as did the senior Orangemen, that it would prove a much more difficult task to deal with unauthorised parades than to marshal duly authorised ones. And so it was. The parades, 100,000 strong, proceeded as usual – although in a rather gloomy atmosphere under grey and leaden skies. With large numbers of RUC and army on standby, however, there was virtually no trouble and the relief of Chichester-Clark and his colleagues, and of Heath and Maudling, was almost tangible. Few could have believed that, in the circumstances, the marches could have gone off so peacefully.

The Republic's External Affairs Minister, Dr Patrick Hillery, had paid an unannounced and, to many, an unwelcome visit that weekend to the Falls Road area which could easily have caused further discontent, but this passed off without much notice and the sense of relief was evident.

In the midst of all the tension over the 12th of July marches, there continued, unabated, similar political tension in unionist party circles. On 8 July, there was a stormy meeting of the Ulster Unionist Standing Committee. There were those who were calling for Chichester-Clark's resignation and those who counselled a more conciliatory approach. Silencing his critics, the Prime Minister recorded a majority in the hall. The chairman, Sir George Clark, summed up by saying that 'there was an appreciation of the fortitude of Major Chichester-Clark and admiration for the way he had faced problems. Lord Craigavon's problems were minimal compared to those facing the present leader'.[16] This certainly seemed like a ringing endorsement for a more and more beleaguered Prime Minister. But, as if to cancel out this more optimistic event, Chichester-Clark soon learnt that one of his staunchest supporters, Anne Dickson, MP for Carrickfergus, had suffered a vote of 'no confidence' passed by her constituency association. However, she declared her determination to stand firm which pleased and encouraged her leader.

A ban on parades

After an Apprentice Boys parade in Londonderry towards the end of July, which had been re-routed to avoid the Bogside area, Chichester-Clark dropped a bombshell. He announced a six month ban on all parades from 23 July until the end of the following January. His decision took most

---

[16] *News Letter,* 9 July 1970

people by complete surprise. 'Peace is at stake here. And so is economic progress and the future of responsible government in Northern Ireland'.[17] The cacophony of disapproving voices was clearly audible. Calls for his resignation abounded; declarations of determination to defy the ban were announced. Chichester-Clark had taken a gamble. The question was – would it work? But before an answer could be given, more senseless violence erupted on the streets of Belfast. For an entire week at the commencement of August, the New Lodge district was at the centre of the mayhem. The army used plastic baton rounds – more commonly known as plastic bullets – for the first time, but it took them days to calm the area sufficiently to let normal life return for the embattled residents. Chichester-Clark could see trouble coming from all sides. The street riots only momentarily took the eyes of the public off the debate on the parades ban. There was, in fact, some confusion over the ban. As it transpired, 'celebrations' were to be permitted but not processions. Whether this was a government sleight of hand or not, it did mean a relaxation of the pressures on the Prime Minister. Whilst it seemed that Chichester-Clark was losing control of many factions within his party, there were some organisations which got him 'off the hook' by saying that 'if the ban is modified to allow traditional parades, Major Chichester-Clark was still "acceptable" as Prime Minister'.[18]

He decided to take a short holiday and headed off to Spain with his wife. Immediately upon his return, looking sun tanned and fit, a crucial meeting of South Londonderry unionists was held in Maghera on 10 August. This meeting is chiefly remembered for the utter confusion which reigned for four hours. Was there a call for Chichester-Clark's resignation? Was there a vote of 'no confidence' in the Government? Some reporters said that Chichester-Clark did not survive a vote of 'no confidence', but others, including the Prime Minister himself, declared that no such vote had taken place. Others said that he had won the vote by 97 votes to 87. The only certainty was that a meeting had taken place and that a large, hostile crowd had caused considerable discomfort to the Prime Minister as he emerged from the hall.

Some days later, on 13 August 1970, Chichester-Clark won the vast majority of support from his Ulster Unionist parliamentary party and from the Senate. Ominously, William Craig, who had been out of Northern

---

[17] *News Letter,* 25 July 1970

[18] *Ibid.,* 4 August 1970

Ireland for two months, raised his head above the parapet and made a bid for the party leadership. Troubles, though, never came singly. On 26 August, the Minister of Home Affairs, Robert Porter, resigned on health grounds. He was undoubtedly one of Chichester-Clark's most resolute supporters and a man he could ill afford to lose from his Cabinet. With immediate effect, the Prime Minister added the Home Affairs portfolio to his responsibilities. He certainly seemed to have reason for doing this for he did not wish to promote Porter's deputy, John Taylor, to the post. He did, however, give Taylor a seat in the Cabinet as Minister of State at Home Affairs – a decision which attracted an amount of opprobrium. Taylor was too closely associated with the group of MPs whose prime object seemed to be to get rid of Chichester-Clark. But the extra responsibility of Home Affairs was most certainly one of the greatest mistakes the Prime Minister had made.

Another lull before another storm

On 21 August, yet another new political party was formed in Northern Ireland. From a diverse group of nationalists and republicans emerged the Social Democratic and Labour Party whose first leader was Gerry Fitt, the Republican Labour MP for West Belfast at Westminster. They numbered six MPs at Stormont at the outset and Fitt declared that the party was 'not just non-sectarian, but actively anti-sectarian'.[19] For his troubles, Fitt was expelled from the Republican Labour Party.

Chichester-Clark shrugged off the formation of this new opposition party but, with the tragic death of a young policeman and the fact that the Royal Black Institution was threatening to defy his ban order, he was ill-equipped to fend off the growing strength of the dissident West Ulster Unionist Council. Although insisting that it was 'not a rebel party, nor a breakaway group',[20] it was certainly a severe challenge to the Chichester-Clark administration. The newspapers considered that the West Ulster Unionists 'have given a clear warning with regard to security, law and order and local government reshaping'.[21]

---

[19] *News Letter,* 22 August 1970

[20] *Ibid.,* 3 September 1970

[21] *Ibid.,* 7 September 1970

Reginald Maudling's second in command at the Home Office, Richard Sharples, visited the Province for four days from 7 September. He had been sent by his boss to sense the real mood in Northern Ireland and he returned to London with the view that, whilst there were clarion calls for Chichester-Clark's resignation, this would neither be in the interest of those in Northern Ireland nor to the government at Westminster. Why Maudling had not come himself to give Chichester-Clark his personal support can only be conjecture. Perhaps it was true what they said about Maudling – 'he was very bright, but idle'. Although Chichester-Clark was on fairly friendly terms with Maudling, the Home Secretary seemed to be trying to distance himself from a place he did not really understand, nor seem to want to.

On 19 September, the unionist party's executive committee passed a vote of 'no confidence' in the Prime Minister's law and order policies. Although there was some confusion as to the legitimacy of the vote when at least half of those entitled to vote were not present, the result – a humiliating defeat by 18 votes to 2 – was a blow to the Prime Minister. Even though it was evident to him that more and more requisitions were arriving at unionist headquarters putting down motions insisting on his resignation, Chichester-Clark seemed to shrug off the pressures. His senses were becoming more and more numb; his sense of direction seemingly more and more haphazard.

During September, the Chief Constable, Sir Arthur Young, who had been in the post for barely one year, announced that he would be leaving the job in November and a senior RUC officer, Graham Shillington, had been appointed to his position. Chichester-Clark paid tribute to Young's work although, inwardly, he had not thought so highly of him. At least the RUC members were happier. They would soon have one of their own men to lead the force.

A storm, of sorts, then arose from a very unusual quarter – an ear infection. It seems incredible to believe that the beginning of the end of a Northern Ireland Prime Minister may have had its foundations in such a seemingly innocuous complaint. Early in October, Chichester-Clark had had a minor ear operation in London. A few days' recovery seemed all that was needed but, as he was recovering, he contracted 'flu and so his absence from work was unavoidably extended. For the best part of two weeks he fought off the various infections and was therefore unable to be present at a number of appointments. These were effectively and competently carried out by John Andrews and Brian Faulkner, although his absence from an important meeting of the Ulster Unionist Standing Conference was critical. Had a vote on his leadership been taken, it would have seemed unlikely that he would have survived it. In the circumstances, and in the absence of Chichester-Clark, Faulkner was able to talk about his various local government reforms and take the heat off the Prime Minister. But he had had a close call and rumours started to circulate. Headlines in local and national newspapers surmised as to the real reasons for Chichester-Clark's prolonged absence. The *Guardian* headline read 'Mr Chichester-Clark's illness has naturally revived speculation over his political future'.[22] The *Daily Mail* affirmed; 'At 46 it is unthinkable that Major Chichester-Clark's ear trouble should cause him to give up the Premiership'.[23] But he had no intention of resigning and, confidently scotching the rumours, he enthusiastically returned to work on 8 October. He received good news and bad news. The good news was that the Ulster Unionist Women had passed a full vote of confidence in the Prime Minister at their annual conference, but the bad news was that violence still stalked the streets of the Province with more riots in Londonderry over the following weekend, 10/11 October.

The ups and downs of his post continued in evidence throughout October. During a visit to Sutton Coldfield, near Birmingham, Chichester-Clark received a very warm welcome and he took the opportunity to try to explain to his English audience how destructive the forces of violence were and how important it was for the law abiding majority to speak up against the terrorists. But a few days later, his South Londonderry constituency officers voted to join the dissident West Ulster Unionist Council. The Prime Minister, as their Member of Parliament, challenged the legitimacy of the vote, and the prospect of his constituency no longer supporting him was 'considered a body blow to Major Chichester-Clark'.[24]

Could the premier's luck be turning?

Chichester-Clark realised that he must take the initiative or all might be lost. So, in a surprise announcement aimed at spiking the guns of the reawakening Civil Rights Association, he told the electorate that he

---

[22] *Guardian,* 30 September 1970

[23] *Daily Mail,* 5 October 1970

[24] *News Letter,* 22 October 1970

intended to introduce 'one man, one vote' with immediate effect. This particular reform had become rather unstuck in recent times and it seemed an opportune time to raise the matter, indicating that its implementation was imminent. Those supporting the Prime Minister, including much of the local press, felt he had made a shrewd move. 'Could it be that Ireland's most enlightened politician is Major Chichester-Clark? It could very well be so. He had taken a very brave stand on the vote. He is allowing one man, one vote in local government by-elections now and over the entire scope of such an election soon'.[25] A number of his supportive backbenchers, like Robert Babington and Basil McIvor, were now actively speaking out against the groundswell of voices calling for the Prime Minister's resignation, namely Harry West and the members of the West Ulster Unionist Council. Such interventions, particularly at this vital time, were most welcome. Although in a difficult position, Chichester-Clark remained optimistic for, regardless of the opposition he was facing from within his own party, he must be credited with the number and relative speed of the many reforms he did introduce. On Maudling's 31 October visit to Belfast, the Prime Minister reminded the Home Secretary of his successes in the extensive reform programme which his government was implementing.

Bernadette Devlin had been released from Armagh prison on 22 October. Might this event avert the Prime Minister's gaze?

Amidst a resilient people – a pause for thought and reflection

During these last years of the Northern Ireland state, there were not just problems for the incumbent Prime Minister; there were horrific times for the people of the Province. In those awful years of the early 1970s, people awoke each day and instinctively switched on their radios. Many had not previously been avid radio listeners, having been more interested in hearing the news on television – in those early days of breakfast time TV. But now radios sat beside almost every bed in Northern Ireland. They were turned on every morning to hear, not if there had been any violent deaths the night before, but just how many there had been. In many instances there might have been as many as 6 or 7 such horrific incidents and the descriptions of these slayings sent a chill through the breasts of the

---

[25] *News Letter*, 3 November 1970

listeners. Things reached the stage that, if there had been no killings, or even just one, an almost audible sigh of relief was heard. Parents arose from their slumbers and, after hearing the latest story of death and destruction, wakened their families and set about their daily routine.

These were the resilient people of Northern Ireland. Life had to go on, slaughter or no slaughter. Husbands and wives set off for work and children and young people left for school. Shops opened, that is if they had not been destroyed the night before, and businesses continued to flourish as best they could. Examination results continued to be every bit as good as in any other place in the British Isles and, in many cases, even better. Youngsters returned home to do their homework and then set out for their evening activities, be that to youth club, Scouts, Boys Brigade or Guides. Parents assisted their younger children with their homework and then made phone calls to their friends and relatives in other parts of Northern Ireland to find out how they had fared in previous nights of terror. Children returned home and went to bed: parents settled their household bills, saw to their home chores, went to bed themselves and waited for the whole process to start again. They woke the next morning, switched on the radio…

At the same time, others went about their business too. These might have been members of the security forces on what they saw as their legitimate business, or members of terrorist organisations who also saw their activity as legitimate business. The cat and mouse game continued apace. Reports came in all day long of police and army arrests of the perpetrators of evil: the actions of the insurgents occurred with monotonous regularity. Who was winning? Was anyone winning?

And in government there was all to play for. With James Chichester-Clark and his family at Castledawson, there was tension and anxiety. There, too, the radio brought the early morning news. The news never seemed encouraging for the Prime Minister, just as it was not good for the ordinary citizens of the Province. Telephone calls had to be made to the seat of government and to police headquarters. Then came the inevitable car journey to Stormont to begin again the work with Cabinet colleagues and civil servants in an attempt to find a solution to the intractable problems of Northern Ireland. There were now additional pressures brought to bear from Westminster. The British government was now, after years of disinterest and inactivity, involved in the day to day matters of the Province. Such intervention had been virtually unknown until just very recently. Northern Ireland had been in the backwater for too long. In recent times it had only just been able to keep afloat. But things were different now and Chichester-Clark had to contend with unwelcome suggestions emanating from London as well as from unhelpful manoeuvres from some of the members of his Cabinet. Life was not a bed of roses for the squire of Moyola Park. It was a life and death struggle in a position which he never really wanted. However he had a job to do and he continued with all the strength he could muster.

Resilience, then, was the watchword – not only for the Prime Minister – but also for the population. It must be said that, had it not been for their resilience and tenacity, the people of Northern Ireland would never have survived. But survive they did.

11

The Final Days of Power

By October 1970, having been Prime Minister for almost 18 months, Chichester-Clark spoke of his sense of individual responsibility in his position as premier and how he also considered that his reforms were commitments of honour. These were bold words coming from a man whose hold on the Prime Minister's position was becoming more tenuous, to say the least. But, although life was still difficult enough, he was beginning to think that things might just be going his way. Commentators were beginning to see Chichester-Clark in a more favourable light. His performances at Stormont were more and more statesmanlike and his handling of the second reading of the Housing Bill on 28 October 1970 was masterly. Although it seemed likely that West and Craig would do their best to sabotage the bill, it went through without a division. Had the tide now turned at last in Chichester-Clark's favour? 'Not so' was the simple answer.

Before November was out, it became clear that a further dissident group of Ulster Unionist MPs could be emerging similar to the troublesome West Ulster Unionist Council, which Harry West had called a 'ginger group' and nothing more sinister. Reputed to be involved in this Belfast group was John Laird, unionist member for St Anne's. He had been elected to the House following the death of his father, who represented this seat for many years and had also been a fierce opponent of Chichester-Clark. The threat of another challenge to Chichester-Clark's authority, with another meeting of the Ulster Unionist Standing Committee due at the beginning of December, was patently unwelcome. Elsewhere in Northern Ireland, the Protestant Unionists attacked Chichester-Clark on law and order. They accused the government of allowing espionage to be carried out in Northern Ireland by agents of the Republic's army. Chichester-Clark forcefully denied this accusation, saying that law and order were in good hands. He demolished his opponents' attack. Then the prospect of further severe confrontations and disturbances reared its ugly head. The Civil Rights Association proposed to march, illegally, in Enniskillen on the last Saturday in November. On the same day, Paisley and his supporters were prepared to put further pressure on the forces of law and order by organising a similar gathering in Armagh. Tension during the preceding week was high but, in the event and with deft use of the 1,000 or so men at their disposal in the two locations, the police and army chiefs were able to ensure that the day went off relatively peacefully. Many demonstrators were arrested and were later convicted of unlawful assembly.

In the succeeding days, Chichester-Clark was asked about the possibility of the introduction of internment. This was, understandably, a delicate and contentious issue to which the Prime Minister responded by saying 'I reserve the right to do whatever may be necessary to protect the security of Northern Ireland'.[1] However it now seemed that such an outcome was becoming a distinct possibility.

On 29 November 1970, Chichester-Clark received some good news. He had been re-elected to the committee of Castledawson unionists who had, just one year earlier, sacked him as a vice president of the local Association. He was now elected president of the branch.

Prior to the meeting of the Ulster Unionist Council Standing Committee, more MPs, like Walter Scott, were appealing for unequivocal support for the Prime Minister. Unity was essential at this critical time. The Council's meeting had been called for 7 December 'to force a showdown between moderates and right-wingers on the divisive issue of the West Ulster Unionist Council's exact role in the party'.[2] As it transpired, the whole affair turned out to be a 'damp squib' and a 'non-event' for, although there were many calls for Harry West and his fellow travellers to be disciplined by the party, no clear-cut decision was taken to do any such thing. It seemed that to thrust the government into more controversy was seen as being most unwise at this time. On the plus side, though, Chichester-Clark did receive a resounding standing ovation, with just a few detractors on this occasion. Perhaps another difficult hurdle had been jumped – perhaps not.

---

[1] *The Times,* 11 December 1970

[2] *News Letter,* 23 November 1970

A State of Emergency

On 7 December, the electricity power station workers took their opportunity to turn the screw on a sensitive government. Having been denied their wage demands from their employers, they decided to go on strike and, before long, many parts of the Province were blacked out. Life quickly became almost impossible for the straightened population and the Governor, Lord Grey, was forced to declare a State of Emergency. For more than a week, old and young suffered equally until, on 14 December, the strikers finally lifted their ban and power was restored to an exasperated people.

As Christmas approached, the government laboured on as manfully as it could. Chichester-Clark and Faulkner were relieved to know that the long-awaited, and much disputed, local government reforms – carefully put together by Patrick McCrory's committee – were within an ace of publication. There continued to be harsh cries of protest from many of the soon-to-be redundant councillors from the proliferation of urban and rural district councils but, by now, the government was prepared to accept the recommendations. Early in 1971, these recommendations would become law thus making the running of local councils much more sensible and meaningful. With the appointment, after just 49 years, of the first Roman Catholic chaplain to Stormont – amidst declarations of pleasure and cries of protests from varying quarters – 1970 came to a close.

For James Chichester-Clark it had been a year of much sorrow and sadness, with some brief glimpses of optimism. What, he thought – as did many others – would 1971 bring? He could approach the new year in the knowledge that there was a strong body of opinion which had given him much credit for proceeding, with more than a fair speed, with many aspects of the reform programme. 'A respectable body of work had been got through'.[3] The Prime Minister remained essentially an optimist, if one who might be beginning to doubt the reasons for his convictions.

1971 looms large

On 12 January, the Prime Minister announced that he intended to make an eight day trip to the United States. He was determined to promote a more

---

[3] Sunday Times Insight Team, *Ulster* (Harmondsworth 1972) p. 234

positive image of Northern Ireland. In the past, Chichester-Clark's predecessor, the globe-trotting Terence O'Neill, had visited the USA on a number of occasions during his spell in office. So Chichester-Clark felt that the time was now right for him to undertake a trip across the Atlantic. He proposed to set off, with his wife, on 17 January. But it was not to be. This Prime Minister was never destined to set foot in North America as Northern Ireland's first citizen. Trouble was brewing yet again at home.

Serious rioting broke out in the Catholic Springfield Road and Ballymurphy areas of Belfast over the weekend 11/12 January. Intensive attacks were made on the security forces on many successive nights and these savage outbreaks, compounded by even more violent escalations in the Protestant Shankill area contemporaneously, had an immediate effect on Chichester-Clark. He summarily cancelled his proposed trip to America and summoned an emergency Cabinet meeting. The situation was ominous and dangerous and many believed that these wintertime incidents had been orchestrated by the men of violence who wanted to see the destruction of the state, the fall of the Chichester-Clark government and the snuffing out of the candle of hope that was to be 'Ulster '71'. These eruptions of firebombing, rioting and killing would, once and for all, ensure that the expected influx of foreign visitors to the celebrations for the 50th anniversary of Northern Ireland would quickly cancel their bookings. And these terrorist elements, in great measure, callously succeeded in their endeavour. The January riots had clearly been 'an evil plot against the 'Ulster '71' exhibition'.[4]

A visit to London to meet the Home Secretary, Reginald Maudling, was speedily arranged for 17 January. Chichester-Clark was accompanied by the Deputy Prime Minister, Senator John Andrews and Brian Faulkner, Minister of Development. The Northern Ireland Ministers sought Maudling's views as how best to control the riots, which were becoming more and more difficult to deal with. The advice proffered was not entirely helpful. Maudling must have seen Chichester-Clark's dilemma, yet he showed a remarkable lack of understanding and a minimal degree of interest. The Northern Ireland premier had, at all times, tried to sort out his own troubles within his jurisdiction and it should have been obvious to the Home Secretary that Chichester-Clark needed assistance. This visit to London 'is an emergency visit which has the aim, metaphorically speaking, of course, of putting a bomb under Mr Maudling. The Ulster

---

[4] *News Letter*, 28 January 1971

Government, far from being prone to panic, normally displays a quite terrifying *sangfroid*. The note of urgency in Major Chichester-Clark's statement yesterday proves how great is the anxiety aroused by last week's riots…Most important of all, however, is the growing feeling, which now threatens Major Chichester-Clark's survival, that life will never return to normal unless swift and drastic action is taken to restore order. Today Major Chichester-Clark should speak out clearly and *Mr Maudling should listen attentively'.*[5] [my emphasis] Typically, Chichester-Clark told his expectant listeners when he arrived back in Belfast that the meeting with Maudling had gone well. It certainly had not. The visit had been 'unrewarding'.[6] Ulster Unionist Westminster MPs, Stratton Mills and Robin Chichester-Clark, protested at the ineffectiveness of London's discharge of its security role by refusing to support the Conservative government in a division in the House. Even so, the future of James Chichester-Clark's premiership was still, without doubt, on the line.

In Belfast the following weekend, 23/24 January, Protestant rioters took to the streets, mainly in the Shankill Road district. Great pressure was brought on Chichester-Clark and his government to deal with this serious situation, in the main from unionist politicians who, whilst condemning the rioting, did little to assuage the problems. Chichester-Clark, in a marathon debate on law and order at Stormont, resolutely refused to give any categorical assurance that internment and curfew would not be introduced. He had to keep all his options open. He was only too aware that recruitment to the RUC and the RUC reserve was slow and both forces were still under strength. At that time, RUC numbers were just 3,745 and the RUC reserve force was badly under its permitted strength of 1,500, with just 642 personnel. Army numbers had long since surpassed the combined numbers in the RUC and its reserve. This information was clearly understood by Ulster Unionist backbenchers, yet they persisted in attacking the Prime Minister remorselessly. 'The Chichester-Clark government was subjected to withering criticism from its own backbenchers'.[7]

It almost went unnoticed that the six month ban on parades had been lifted on 31 January – a decision which surprised not a few and pleased many others.

---

[5] *Daily Telegraph,* 18 January 1971

[6] *Irish Press,* 19 January 1971

[7] *News Letter,* 28 January 1971

There was yet further trouble on the horizon for the embattled Prime Minister. Over 150 leading unionists called for an emergency meeting of the Ulster Unionist Council, that unwieldy body of unionists representing officials and rank and file members from all parts of the Province. It would only have taken 30 members to submit such a requisition for the meeting to be called and the only discretion for the officials was that they could delay its date until some time in the future. The reason for the call was that James Chichester-Clark and his government seemed incapable of maintaining law and order on the streets of Northern Ireland.

Violence continues on the streets of Belfast

Whilst this clamouring for the resignation of the Prime Minister continued almost unabated, a rumour emerged that the Speaker, Major Ivan Neill, had been mentioned as a possible successor to Chichester-Clark – if he resigned. As it transpired, this report was totally without foundation.

Burnings and shootings continued with monotonous regularity on the streets of the Province. In early February, the scenes of the worst disturbances were in the Kashmir Road area of Belfast. But 5 February 'was one of the grimmest and most tragic nights in the history of the capital'.[8] During that night the first British soldier to be killed in the present troubles was gunned down in Belfast. He was Gunner Robert Curtis, a young married man, just 20 years old. Shockwaves permeated the entire Province and further afield. Chichester-Clark was appalled and went on television the next day to appeal, once more, for common sense to prevail in these most dreadful circumstances. He made his position abundantly clear in his broadcast. 'Northern Ireland is at war with the IRA Provisionals'.[9] He enlisted the support of Church and other community leaders to keep their localities calm. The murder of soldiers and other members of the security forces was now becoming almost commonplace and hijackings and destruction of property became the staple diet for regular readers of the local newspapers. Chichester-Clark loudly and consistently declared that

---

[8] *News Letter,* 6 February 1971
[9] *Ibid.,* 8 February 1971

his government would never surrender to Irish republicans and other terrorists.

Chichester-Clark was becoming more and more conscious that his government's law and order policies were constantly under fire, and often from members of his own party. He knew that opponents of his policies fully intended to criticise him at a forthcoming meeting of the Ulster Unionist Council. He made it clear that he would resign if a majority of delegates proved to be against him. He was being assailed from all sides. He could see that he was now, in cricketing parlance, almost always 'on the back foot'. He desperately looked around for a breathing space.

This came from an unexpected source. The Taoiseach, Jack Lynch, who had caused the Prime Minister some considerable trouble the previous August, now seemed to give some support to the Northern Ireland government. He made strong public statements condemning the IRA for their vicious attacks on people and property in the north. In response, Chichester-Clark welcomed the Irish Prime Minister's clear and unambiguous statement. He felt that his erstwhile remarks against the southern government's interference in Northern Ireland's affairs had borne fruit. But the northern population had long forgotten the beleaguered Prime Minister's earlier strident interventions.

Murder most horrid

The dastardly and calculated murder of five electricity workers, who were blown up and killed as they travelled in a Land Rover up Brougher Mountain on the Tyrone and Fermanagh border on their way to repair a transmitter on 9 February 1971, caused revulsion throughout the community. The Prime Minister utterly condemned this act of barbarity and declared that these 'forces of evil' in the community would be rooted out. In the aftermath of this atrocity, and other similar ones, the Stormont government determined to increase the strength of the Special Powers Act. In recent times the IRA had become ever more audacious, even appearing at funerals wearing uniforms and concealing their dead and injured. There were occasions when they buried their dead in the middle of the night. Chichester-Clark and his government were determined to stamp out this type of illegal activity. Legislation was, therefore, quickly passed in the House of Commons, although not without opposition from nationalist MPs and members of the SDLP. Chichester-Clark felt that the fact that he had taken such speedy and resolute action would improve his standing. But this was not to be.

Over the weekend 13/14 February, Chichester-Clark, accompanied by his wife but none of his Cabinet colleagues, travelled to England where he had talks at Chequers on the Northern Ireland situation with the British Prime Minister, Edward Heath, and a number of his closest senior Cabinet colleagues. Chichester-Clark updated the British Ministers on the ever-worsening security situation in the Province. Heath offered support and further measures to assist the ailing Northern Ireland economy. But this was cold comfort to Chichester-Clark. He needed more concrete proposals from Heath, which were not exactly forthcoming. He returned to Belfast in a sombre mood. He did not have much to tell the baying mob. The Stormont government would have to try to get on with the difficult task of coping with the ever-increasing security problems. He now tried to calm the unionists' fears over the constitution and firmly declared that there would be no change and the links with the Crown would remain as strong as ever.

Chichester-Clark continued to try to make life more normal for the citizens of Northern Ireland. 1971 was the 50th anniversary of the state of Northern Ireland, a fact largely forgotten amidst the troubles faced by society. Although all its citizens would not have been overjoyed to be reminded of this, nonetheless, arrangements were well in hand to celebrate this event. The Prime Minister, along with very many business men and women and well known sports personalities, was doing his best to promote 'Ulster '71'. He spoke out enthusiastically about the benefits of the celebrations and various advertisements appeared on television and in the press to 'give a positive spin' to the forthcoming fun and games, which were to commence in May and go on until August. He asserted that 'confidence that the differences in our community will be healed – that is what 'Ulster '71' is all about'.[10] But would people, especially those from abroad, take any heed of his exhortations?

By mid February, with the ban on parades now lifted, the Civil Rights Association decided to take to the streets once again. They arranged a march from Coalisland to Dungannon for 20 February and it was certain that this would be a test of the government's 'normalisation' policy. A large number of the security forces was on duty that day but, much to the relief of

---

[10] *News Letter,* 17 February 1971

the Prime Minister, his Cabinet and the security forces, the march passed off peacefully.

Earlier in February, William, Cardinal Conway had condemned the murderous actions of the IRA. This was good news for the government and showed to extreme loyalist politicians that the head of the Roman Catholic Church was prepared to denounce such action unequivocally, even when it came from those who, at least tenuously, belonged to his church. On 25 February, a momentous event took place. For the first time, James Chichester-Clark and Cardinal Conway met in the Prime Minister's office at Stormont. They held informal talks about relationships within the community and both men declared how useful the meeting had been. Over the next few months, unknown to most people, the Cardinal and the Prime Minister had a number of further private, and equally helpful, meetings. Each seemed to like the other, but public reaction was mixed – and predictable. Most people, however, approved of the Prime Minister's decision to meet with the man who held considerable sway within his community. It had been a good publicity exercise. To many Catholics, Chichester-Clark was now seen as a much less unionist orientated man and saw him as someone prepared to talk and listen to the Catholic side of affairs. But Chichester-Clark had not long to reap the rewards of this reasonable and decent act. The Young Unionists were now baying for his blood, egged on by the Prime Minister's archenemy, William Craig.

At the Ulster Hall on 1 March, a large gathering of the Young Unionists met. The majority of those in the hall gave William Craig a standing ovation when he called for the resignation of Chichester-Clark and his government. Craig was in his element, basking in the glow of the resounding cheers of so many Young Unionists. It was to be these echoes of support that were to bring more and more glory and acclamation to William Craig, at least for a few more short months. He was, in the end, however, soon to be consigned to the political scrap heap. Chichester-Clark's reaction to the calls of the Young Unionists was simply to ignore them and get on with the business of governing. This additional mounting pressure on Chichester-Clark was, as ever, most unwelcome.

In parliament, debates were lively and the backbenchers' clarion calls continued without ceasing. The Prime Minister was attacked on the perceived slackness and inefficiency of his administration. By early March, Chichester-Clark had introduced more security measures to ensure that the army was given power to be ever present in IRA terrorist enclaves and to introduce the policy of 'hot pursuit'. Yet the onslaught from a number of the backbench unionists, such as Joseph Burns, Robert Mitchell, Harry West and others, continued unabated. They persisted in their call for the re-arming of the RUC and the introduction of more effective measures to support the forces of law and order. Chichester-Clark's hold on the members of his own party was loosening.

He could hardly control his sense of disgust and revulsion when, on 26 February, two members of the RUC were shot dead during disturbances in the Ardoyne area of Belfast. It now became one of the more shocking realities of life in Northern Ireland for Cabinet Ministers, and the Prime Minister himself, to dutifully follow the sad corteges of many murdered servants of the Crown. In double quick time, and for the first time in over a year, some members of the police force were re-armed. They had barely time to adjust when fierce fighting broke out again at Unity Flats in west Belfast, occasioning yet more senseless violence.

Reginald Maudling visits the Province

After much media hype, the British Home Secretary, Reginald Maudling, visited Northern Ireland for three days starting on 4 March. He took the almost unprecedented step of speaking to the combined Houses of Commons and Senate in the Great Hall at Stormont. He commended the RUC, the Northern Ireland government and the decent people of the Province for their tenacity and resolve against the forces of evil at work in the community. But this was not enough for the assembled MPs and Senators. They wanted to hear of more positive action which they felt that the British government must take. They wanted action on additional security measures soon. They were dismissive of Maudling's reassurances and left Stormont that day in a very disgruntled mood. They had wanted to hear Maudling say that the UDR would be fully integrated into the army. They had wanted to hear him say that their numbers would be increased. They had wanted to see the Home Secretary show a more determined approach to the ever-escalating violence in this part of Her Majesty's realm. But they had heard none of these reassurances. They were decidedly unhappy and concerned. Maudling spent the remainder of his visit talking to churchmen, Trades Unionists and other politicians but, when he left, his departure went unnoticed. The people of Northern Ireland realised that they just had to get on with it.

Chichester-Clark, although outwardly appreciative of the Home Secretary's mild support, felt, in his heart, much the same as everyone else. Reginald Maudling had failed to deliver in a life and death situation.

The situation continues to deteriorate

A most spine chilling atrocity took place just outside Belfast on 10 March. Three young Scottish soldiers, two of them brothers and only in their early twenties, were lured to their deaths by evil men. They had been out for an evening's enjoyment when they were abducted and brutally murdered. Their bodies were dumped, ignominiously, on a lonely hillside outside Belfast. As soon as the news of this monstrous deed was made known, utter shock was expressed by all. Chichester-Clark and every other MP at Stormont, when solemnly debating the effects of this depravity, were angry, incensed and infuriated. The IRA itself even had the gall to say that there had been no need for these young soldiers to have been killed. This empty rhetoric broke no ice in Scotland where sorrowing parents and families laid these fine young men to rest.

There were now calls for immediate action. Many backbenchers were calling for internment to be quickly introduced. In private, even Cabinet members felt that there was no alternative to this fateful move. On Friday 12 March, Chichester-Clark, feeling the pressure even more acutely, called an emergency meeting of the Cabinet and the GOC, General Harry Tuzo,* was summoned to attend. There was one question above all others addressed to the general. If internment was introduced, would it work and would the forces be able to enforce this drastic action? These were tough and searching questions to the man who, after all, was simply the servant of his political masters. Internment could be made to work but speed and secrecy were of the essence if the outcome was to be effective. There were too many possibilities for leaks of information. The members of the IRA and the other subversive organisations probably had too many chances to evade capture. That same evening a delegation of high-ranking Trades Unionists came to meet the Prime Minister. They were filled with determination to ensure that Chichester-Clark and his Cabinet members

---

* Tuzo had only recently taken over command after the sudden illness of General Erskine Crum, who himself had just recently succeeded General Freeland. Sadly General Crum died on 17 March, just a few days later.

were left in no doubt that positive action of the kind mentioned was absolutely necessary. They understood the Prime Minister's dilemma, but they told him, in no uncertain terms, that their members, who after all represented a large majority of the Province's workers, were at the end of their tether. They demanded action against the terrorists who were clearly threatening their livelihoods. Their leaders were impressed by Chichester-Clark's obvious determination not to let them down. They understood his problems, and, although they did not unnecessarily want to make his situation worse, they insisted on a speedy way forward.

Out in the country, there continued to be concentrated and vicious attacks on Chichester-Clark. While he was quite well used to these pressures, the Prime Minister now faced prolonged and organised moves to have votes of 'no confidence' passed in what many local associations saw as his inability to run Northern Ireland. 'The political career of Major Chichester-Clark hangs in the balance today. From all quarters he is being harangued. He is used to that. Northern Ireland is not known for its moderation. Major Chichester-Clark is in an uneasy, ironical and unenviable position'.[11] He seemed to have few friends and supporters and, accustomed as he was to unfriendly resolutions, he could only take so much. The next meeting of the Ulster Unionist Council was scheduled for 29 March. Chichester-Clark could only dread this gathering with foreboding. To meet upwards of 800 delegates, many of whom would certainly be baying for his blood, did not fill him with confidence. He was now firmly in a corner, from which escape seemed more and more unlikely.

A final attempt to make London see sense

Early that following week Chichester-Clark, without any direct consultation with his colleagues, set off for a visit to London. This unexpected visit came rather as a surprise to all those close to the beleaguered Prime Minister. Something needed to be done, but a London visit did not seem 'on the cards' at that particular time.

But Chichester-Clark felt that 'it was now or never'. He was determined to put his case to Heath and Maudling once and for all. He needed more troops in Northern Ireland, and he needed them immediately.

---

[11] *News Letter,* 15 March 1971

Any time for procrastination had passed. If the Province in general, and its Prime Minister and its government in particular, was to survive, nothing short of a substantial increase in the army complement was urgently required. It was 'make or break' time for Northern Ireland. He had made up his mind that if extra troops of the numbers he was proposing were not forthcoming, he would have no alternative but to resign the premiership. The figure which Chichester-Clark had in mind was an immediate increase of 3,000 troops. Although this would represent a considerable increase in the number of available land forces, he felt the request was necessary to make an all out effort to rid the Province of the IRA terror. Having listened to Chichester-Clark's demands, Reginald Maudling made a very serious error in judgement. It was one he would live to regret. He offered just 1,300 additional troops. He clearly either felt that Chichester-Clark's request was unrealistic or that the Northern Irish Prime Minister was trying to get Westminster to do his dirty work. In any event, Maudling turned down the request and Chichester-Clark returned to Belfast in high dudgeon. He was now determined to let someone else take on the thankless task of being the Prime Minister of Northern Ireland at this dangerous and critical time. He felt thoroughly let down by the British establishment and, although many of his closest friends and colleagues implored him not to take any drastic action, he had made up his mind. The Belfast morning newspaper noted, with an air of despondency, that 'the Prime Minister is disillusioned and very frustrated'.[12]

When Edward Heath, having heard from his Home Secretary soon after Chichester-Clark's return to Belfast, realised what was likely to happen, he appealed to Chichester-Clark not to take the action he threatened. With the rising speculation in the local Belfast papers that the Prime Minister was on the point of resignation, Heath sent Lord Carrington, with all speed, across to the Province on the morning of Saturday 20 March 1971 with orders to retrieve the situation if at all possible. But it was too late. The die was cast for James Chichester-Clark. Although he put off his final decision for hours on that fateful Saturday, the end came late that day. After just 689 days as Northern Ireland's Prime Minister, James Chichester-Clark tendered his resignation to the Governor, Lord Grey of Naunton, and the Governor accepted his resignation with regret.

---

[12] *News Letter,* 20 March 1971

In his message to the population of Northern Ireland, James Chichester-Clark remained dignified. There was no rancour in the words which he expressed. He declared that he had done his level best for the people and finished off by saying that 'I would only add my warmest thoughts to all those who have supported me during the time in which I have had the honour to head the government of Northern Ireland'.[13] Many were undoubtedly happy, and even overjoyed, at the turn of events but the majority of the population hung its head in shame. Even John Andrews and Brian Faulkner were moved to offer to resign with Chichester-Clark, a suggestion which he immediately scotched. Some had accused Chichester-Clark of deserting the sinking ship, but had these very people not been those who had hounded him into taking this step? History alone will tell whether the action taken by James Chichester-Clark that Saturday 20 March 1971 was correct.

---

[13] *News Letter,* 22 March 1971

12

Success or Failure?

And so, after 689 days or 22 months or 98 weeks, the short-lived premiership of James Chichester-Clark came to an end. The decision to resign was taken quickly and there could be no prevarication. This was the mark of Chichester-Clark. His mind was made up and, rather than unnecessarily putting off the evil day and subjecting the Province to further speculation, he resigned, leaving those in charge of filling the vacancy to the task in hand. In his own mind he had done a reasonable job – perhaps it had not been spectacular – but it had been an honest attempt to ensure the betterment of all who lived in Northern Ireland and the expulsion of the terrorist menace. His sense of powerlessness was clearly evident.

Many books written on this period in Northern Ireland's history are smattered with off-hand remarks about the premiership of James Chichester-Clark. Many of these comments are brief, inaccurate and decidedly unreasonable. Others are damned with faint praise. Yet more are curt and negative. But passing comments and 'off the cuff' references on such an important personage as a Prime Minister of Northern Ireland in biographies of others do not portray the true picture of the man. These other authors could be forgiven for concentrating on their own subjects but omissions and misconceptions about this honourable man must be redressed.

It is pertinent to examine some of the references in other books as to the main reasons for Chichester-Clark's resignation. There are a number which are relatively positive or at least not too negative. '(Chichester-Clark's) government had allowed itself to be brought down by a combination of civil rights cajolery and British wimpishness'.[1] 'He must be

---

[1] P. Arthur and K. Jeffrey, *Northern Ireland since 1968* (Oxford 1989) p. 54

the only person who had to resign in politics to make people understand what he had meant while in office'.[2] 'There is a good deal of irony, in retrospect, in the fact that Britain brought Chichester-Clark down because he was too demanding'.[3] These quotations show Chichester-Clark in a rather different light. It seems clear that his position vis a vis the British government was one of determination and not of weakness. James Chichester-Clark never 'cried wolf' for he knew what Northern Ireland needed in its hour of greatest need. It was the Tory government which did not listen and ignored the measured requests of their man on the ground.

Some references do, however, take a decidedly negative stance. Brian Faulkner, who worked well with Chichester-Clark and who grew more and more to respect him, insists that 'Chichester-Clark was determined to go'.[4] David Bleakley, soon to be a Minister in Faulkner's government, declares that 'Chichester-Clark staggered on manfully for 22 months, comprehending little and enjoying nothing of the political disaster in which he was involved'.[5] Professor Joe Lee writes (after Heath had refused to give Chichester-Clark the troops he had requested) 'When Heath refused, the hapless Clarke(sic) brought his somnambulatory premiership to a close'.[6] It is eminently obvious that these men have taken the view, as expressed in the references above, that Chichester-Clark spent his time in a kind of sleep-walking daze doing a job for which he had no ability nor any interest. This is not the truth. Such sweeping statements, some of which emanate from men who were not directly involved in the helter-skelter of life in those difficult and dangerous years, do little justice to those who made them. They fail to recognise the actual and physical difficulties and strains under which Chichester-Clark, and the others in his administration, was suffering.

Why did this gentle giant of a man ever take on this poisoned chalice? The answer, like most in the intricate affairs of politics, is never easy to discover. When Terence O'Neill could cope no longer in April 1969 and resigned, there certainly was some unravelling to be done and some serious intrigue to be untangled. Had O'Neill resigned because he was past listening to those who were his advisors? Was he so 'gutted' after the

---

[2] Henry Kelly, *How Stormont Fell* (Dublin 1972) p. 14

[3] Sunday Times Insight Team, *Ulster* (Harmondsworth 1972) p. 251

[4] Brian Faulkner, *Memoirs of a Statesman* (London 1978) p. 75

[5] David Bleakley, *Faulkner* (Oxford 1974) p. 77

[6] J.J. Lee, *Ireland 1912-1985* (Cambridge 1989) p. 435

seemingly hopeful signs of his 'Crossroads' speech had been dispelled in the uncertain results of the general election? Did Ian Paisley's now famous and resounding retort (after hearing the Bannside result) of "Let me smell that man's breath" finally bring home to him that the divisive politics in Northern Ireland were not for an aristocrat such as he? Did he realise that his reform programme was not, after all, exactly the path he wanted to pursue? Chichester-Clark, rather than somehow drifting into the Prime Ministerial race, had made up his mind positively to force O'Neill's resignation. As a close confidant of O'Neill's, it was a tricky position to be in. But Chichester-Clark had become infuriated with O'Neill for, in recent times, the man never seemed to listen to him nor take his advice. O'Neill's image of being the shy person who only confided in a few, now became the man who listened to none. This was untenable for a man holding such an important public office. Therefore, in Chichester-Clark's estimation, O'Neill had 'shot his bolt'. Although 'Terence had some good years',[7] he could no longer be trusted with the leadership of Northern Ireland and, with the support of many, and especially of his brother, Robin, the man from Moyola Park pressed his claim. At home, his decision was not popular but he felt it his bounden duty to try to attain the post now certain to become vacant.

James Chichester-Clark had never any burning ambition to become Prime Minister. He had not spent sleepless nights as a young man giving thought to Prime Ministerial speeches and the formation of Cabinets. He knew that such ambitions would be frowned upon at home. So why did he proceed? Knowing that O'Neill was about to go, he keenly felt his sense of duty. For what it was worth, O'Neill himself had made contact with Chichester-Clark and had encouraged him to put his name 'into the ring'. In the prevailing circumstances, he simply felt that it would be entirely appropriate to follow the long line of illustrious political ancestors and so he decided to press his claim. He knew that others with different ideas would oppose him, but, in the end, and by that excruciatingly narrow margin of one, he succeeded in his mission. He was Prime Minister of Northern Ireland, something almost as insecure in 1969 as being the leader of a breakaway Russian state in the late 1990s.

Being a Prime Minister of Northern Ireland in the 1940s and 1950s represented to its holder a certain amount of power and prestige. Perhaps not too much of either of these attributes, but just enough to bask in some

---

[7] *Belfast Telegraph,* 1 June 1992

element of glory. To be a Prime Minister of Northern Ireland in the late 1960s and 1970s was an entirely different matter. Terence O'Neill's ship of state had been buffeted by the winds of change but James Chichester-Clark's was, more often than not, to be smashed against the jagged cliffs in the midst of a mighty torrent. How did he steer the ship off the rocks? The answer, without a doubt, is – with varying degrees of difficulty.

'Behind the granite face there was a likeable man, as honourable as they come, and one capable of inspiring trust'.[8] These attributes describe a man who has been underestimated and misjudged by the majority in so many passing, ill thought out references and oblique remarks. A man of patent honesty and immense courage, Chichester-Clark set out on the path as Prime Minister with wisdom and determination. He nicely wrong-footed his detractors when he effected an amnesty for Paisley, Bunting and others when he undertook his post. It was almost a stroke of genius. Nor did he shy away from talking to his opponents, even when their language was nothing short of 'nautical'. He showed courage on the occasions when he faced the crowds at the peace lines and, even for a time, gained their respect. However, he was never a good broadcaster. He spoke on television many times and rarely acquitted himself well. The silver screen held no attractions for him. But he was not alone in finding that exposure to the media was a daunting task. He was never a whinger, preferring to make do with what he had, rather than passing round the begging bowl at Westminster as one of his predecessors, Lord Craigavon, was wont to do. Many expected him to be a tedious debater in the Stormont House of Commons, but his speeches were, on many occasions, incisive and to the point. His delivery was competent and straightforward and his discourses sharp. He did, of course, have great assistance in speech writing from his worthy civil servants, but it was he who had to deliver them – whether in the House of Commons or in some tiny Orange Hall in the heart of the countryside. And he, although not exactly relishing the prospect, managed many vitriolic encounters with hecklers and dissidents with a certain amount of ease and aplomb.

During his term of office, Chichester-Clark was required to attend meetings of the Ulster Unionist Council, and its committees, with unremitting regularity. It was a fearsome task to have to explain one's government's programmes to this motley gathering of sometimes 300 and often up to 800 people. Many of these meetings were difficult to handle.

---

[8] Ken Bloomfield, *Stormont in Crisis – a Memoir* (Belfast 1994) p. 73

There were usually diverse views expressed and many of these could be quite abusive. Delegates from all parts of the Province had their own likes and dislikes, their own complaints and grouses and they cared little about putting their Prime Minister on the spot. Although Chichester-Clark sometimes felt the glow of a standing ovation, more often as not during his premiership, he felt the chilling reality of close votes, sit down protests and censorious hand clapping. In truth, these Ulster Unionist Council meetings became more and more difficult for him to face. He lost a dubious vote of confidence on one occasion, missed another crucial meeting at the beginning of October 1970 because of the after-effects of an ear operation and only escaped the grasps of a even more formidable assembly by resigning on 20 March 1971. He was certainly more than relieved to have no more such unhappy gatherings to attend. It had never been his favourite place to be.

The true attitude to reform

Chichester-Clark's attitude to the reform programme does need a fuller examination. The myth that he resigned as Minister of Agriculture because of the timing of the 'one man, one vote' reform has now been, once and for all, dispelled. He knew that O'Neill had to go and, once he had resigned, there were those who wondered what Chichester-Clark's attitude to the reform programme was going to be. The answer quickly came when the new Prime Minister not only immediately processed that very reform over which the dispute had been – the 'one man, one vote' issue – but also brought his most able Minister, and his recent opponent, Brian Faulkner, into the Ministry of Development to guide the most difficult reforms through Stormont. Had Chichester-Clark not been such a visionary, he could have appointed a colleague to that Ministry whose efforts to pursue the necessary reforms might not have been sufficiently vigorous. Brian Faulkner was the man for the job, being a hard worker and one who, at this early stage at any rate, was willing to show his premier that he was prepared to put country before self interest. Chichester-Clark swiftly brought in the legislation to reform the cumbersome local council arrangements and to introduce the unitary housing authority. Faulkner then set about implementing this long and difficult process with the zeal and assiduousness for which he was renowned. At all times the Prime Minister gave his colleague full and unconditional support, both in the cockpit of Stormont and also in the local lions' dens – the small halls throughout the Province where debate on local government and housing reform was fought tooth and nail.

Chichester-Clark liked the 'B' Specials. He felt that they had done a good job throughout the years, often in trying circumstances. He knew that they had their 'bad apples' and said so. Given more time it seems certain that a review of the police would have been a priority for him. When the Hunt Report was set up, however, he knew then that changes would be recommended for there had been too many occasions of late when members of the Specials had let the force down. The RUC did need modernisation in order to improve its image in society and the Prime Minister, whilst wishing that the main thrust for reform of the constabulary had come from his government alone, did go out of his way to support the principal recommendations of Hunt. The phasing out of the 'B' Specials was, of course, the most controversial of those recommendations and the one which caused most anguish throughout the Province. Chichester-Clark had to deal with the resultant opprobrium and the constant threats of resignation from force members, taking much of it fairly and squarely on his own broad shoulders, and yet he took the matter forward with consummate ardour. As the time went on he assured many of the former loyal 'B' Specials that there was a place for them either in the new RUC reserve force or in the Ulster Defence Regiment. In due course, both these new forces came into being and the Prime Minister was always around to publicly speak out in their support and to ensure that both sides of the community would be represented in them. There was but limited success in his admirable endeavours for, although there were plenty of applications to join, the numbers from the minority population still remained lower than had been hoped and expected.

The topic of reform was always brought up when Chichester-Clark had his all too frequent meetings with the British Prime Minister and members of his Cabinet. They wanted to know how the reforms were progressing; they were anxious to determine the dates when necessary legislation would be passed at Stormont; they insisted that this matter was for ever at the top of every agenda. The Ulster premier reassured firstly, Wilson and Callaghan, then Heath and Maudling, that the laws were finding their way on to the statute book with amazing speed. It was fair to say that Chichester-Clark soon wearied of the rantings of British officials on the issue of reform. He was too much of a gentleman to remind them that, during his term of office at the helm of Northern Ireland's affairs, he and his government had processed more reforming legislation than any previous holder of the post – a fact which few have ever appreciated.

In the end, one has to ask the question – did James Chichester-Clark really believe in his own reform package? Was he a convinced reformer or was he just being constantly pushed by one or other of the persistent occupants of 10 Downing Street? Although not easy questions to answer, it has to be said that there were certainly some hints of reticence in Chichester-Clark's mind as he was hastening from one reform to another. During its 50 year old history, no one in the state of Northern Ireland ever showed any great enthusiasm to bring the minority into the full reins of office. In many ways one can see the reasons for their reluctance to open up the establishment to those who would have openly been unsupportive of the state. And it can hardly be said that Craigavon, Andrews and Brookeborough had any great taste for reform. They did not even consider it. They did not see the need for it. Their job, as they saw it, was to ensure the future for an Ulster Unionist hegemony and they succeeded in their narrow minded task. When it came to Terence O'Neill, things changed. He began to acknowledge that there were those in society who had never been involved in the running of it. Given that they would support the constitution of Northern Ireland, he was prepared to bring them close to the periphery of power. But by 1968, O'Neill had given up. Perhaps his cover had been blown. Perhaps he was not a genuine reformer after all. By early 1969, he was tired of power and, in the middle of his years in office, had even declared that he only ever wanted to be Prime Minister for six years or so anyway. On the positive side, however, it should be remembered that it was O'Neill who did look forward as none of his predecessors had done before him. A programme of expanding Northern Ireland's industries had been, in large measure, successful. He had stretched out a hand of friendship to a southern Prime Minister. He had at least prised open the door of reform for his successor to enter in.

At the beginning of a new millennium, when so much has happened since Good Friday 1998, it may seem that the reforms initiated by Chichester-Clark or somehow imposed on him in those pioneering days of the late 1960s and early 1970s, are the actual foundations of what we are experiencing today. This is indeed the case. Chichester-Clark did believe in reform. He recognised the disasters of the past and wanted to show that he was up to the challenge of effecting reforms which would bring Northern Ireland right into the present age. He was partially successful. He would have been infinitely more successful had he been given the unequivocal support of all his parliamentary colleagues and of that dreaded body, the Ulster Unionist Council. It is facile and naïve, nonetheless, to apportion total guilt to those around Chichester-Clark without saying that his own staying power may well also have been in question. Had he remained in power longer and 'slugged it out' with his opponents, the future might have been different. But he had come against an immovable object in the form of the British government which was never really attuned to the vagaries of this outpost of the United Kingdom. They were not able to appreciate the immense difficulties facing their own man – James Chichester-Clark – and they failed to support him. He therefore resigned, hoping against hope, that his successor would have more luck in his quest for a brighter future for the citizens of Northern Ireland. His chief reason for resignation, he would declare, was because he had lost the support of his constituents who had elected him MP for South Londonderry. 'If my own people don't support me, why should I go on'?[9] For this essentially domestic reason, in addition to those ascribed to him by the weighty power-broking debates between Prime Ministers, James Chichester-Clark left office. He felt he had run out of real choices and saw no point in going on. That door, prised open by O'Neill, had been pushed a little further ajar by Chichester-Clark.

Significant events of a tormented premiership

In recording such a tumultuous term of office, it seems only right and proper to highlight the events which influenced Chichester-Clark's time as Prime Minister. By drawing together these following events, it will be clear that about a dozen or so matters shaped his premiership. Mostly they caused him pain, discomfort and even embarrassment, but they taught him much. The cruel events of the Bogside riots signalled impending doom for the Province. When the troops had to be brought in, the first dismantling of the power of Stormont was evident, at least as far as security was concerned. The seemingly deliberate statement by Harold Wilson about the imminent disbanding of the 'B' Specials drove Chichester-Clark into a corner from which it became almost impossible to break out. He had been betrayed at probably the most crucial episode in Northern Irish history. He

---

[9] *Conversation with Lord Moyola*, 1 December 1999

had been on the back foot ever since and found it exceedingly difficult to get on to a firm footing again.

The fact that he had to deal with three reports about vital affairs of state – the Cameron, Hunt and Scarman reports – would have been too much for any Prime Minister, regardless of his ability and experience, to stomach. Yet, to his everlasting credit, Chichester-Clark managed all three with a degree of tenacity. Although the 'B' Specials were to be disbanded, he was able to focus his attention on the need to encourage men and women to enlist in the defence of Northern Ireland by joining the new forces.

He liked James Callaghan, but he was pushed around by him – maybe not in a deliberate way – but in a way that Callaghan was able to show him who was boss. The change of government, from Labour to Conservative in June 1970, was an unwanted intrusion for Chichester-Clark, yet he rode out this storm of change with great level-headedness. He might often have wished to have had the pushy Callaghan once again in exchange for the disinterested Maudling. The two British Prime Ministers during his administration, Harold Wilson and Edward Heath, showed not only a disregard for the difficulties under which Chichester-Clark was languishing, but also an exasperation in having to face up to the seemingly intractable problems affecting the Province. In his comments following the Bogside riots, Wilson expressed his misguided irritation at what he saw as the intransigence of the Northern Ireland government. 'It was also the culmination of nearly fifty years of the unimaginative inertia and repression of successive, unchallenged, and, because of Ulster's history, unchallengeable, Ulster Unionist Governments'.[10] Heath, similarly, demonstrated his 'overlordship' of Chichester-Clark with his view of how the July 1970 parades ban was brought about. 'I therefore insisted that Chichester-Clark should ban sectarian parades until the end of January'.[11] The Ulster premier had, of course, the thoroughly opposing point of view.

Party squabbles at the Ulster Unionist Council, amongst the dissident west Ulster group of MPs or within his own constituency associations, often caused him to be weary and despondent. Taking on the post of Minister of Home Affairs, when Porter resigned in August 1970, was a mistake but, at the time, he had little alternative.

---

[10] Harold Wilson, *The Labour Government 1964-1970 – a Personal Record* (London 1971) p. 692

[11] Edward Heath, *The Autobiography of Edward Heath – The Course of my Life* (London 1998) p. 425

There were two circumstances which troubled Chichester-Clark most of all and they were to be the most significant of his Prime Ministerial career. They were the 'no-go' areas and, as he saw it, the real underlying and root problem of Northern Ireland's society – community discontent. Many people, including members of the security forces, watched the 'no-go' areas and the barricades go up without any foresight as to what might be the consequences. They simply thought that, in due course of time, the barriers would come down and life would return to normal. James Chichester-Clark saw it quite differently. As soon as he saw one such area start to flourish, he realised what was happening. The local population would be intimidated by a burgeoning and ever confident IRA and the forces of law and order would perhaps never be able to return. It was, in Chichester-Clark's eyes, absolutely vital to remove the barricades at once. If this had been done, then the influence of the IRA – and also of Protestant para-militaries – would have been severely diminished, if not eradicated. But he could not get others to heed his 'cris de coeur' and these areas persisted, resulting in the haemorrhaging of a right and just society for all.

'Chichester-Clark was among the optimists of Ulster – he could, by mid 70 – see that "communal discontent" was the fundamental problem for Northern Ireland – not the IRA'.[12] The discontent shown by many people manifested itself when those of the minority population began to realise the disadvantages from which they suffered. They rightfully saw poor housing, a greater degree of unemployment and gerrymandered council areas as matters which severely affected their prospects in life. The emergence of the Civil Rights Association started to marshal their thoughts – and their forces. Unionist governments were unused to street protests. O'Neill had made an amount of progress to right the wrongs, but many in the minority now wanted a more rapid improvement of their lot. They looked to the new Prime Minister, Chichester-Clark. Many were not hopeful that another of the landed unionist classes who had attained the heights of Prime Ministerial rank would do any better than his predecessors. Many were to be genuinely surprised. James Chichester-Clark, whilst not a born reformer, had every intention of proceeding with reforms already in the pipeline. Brushing aside any doubts which he may have had, he boldly passed law after law to give equal rights to all. He saw that 'communal discontent' existed. He could see and understand the reasons for it and he was convinced reforms should continue apace. But he

---

[12] Sunday Times Insight Team, *Ulster* (Harmondsworth 1972) p. 230

was wallowing in a sea of unionist intransigence. He had to fight off revolt after revolt to ensure that the ship of reform was not dashed against the rocks of obduracy. He knew he was moving in the right direction but even he could not counter the mass of disturbance blocking his way.

There were those who had appreciated what he had achieved during his time in office. 'He is a man of whom all who value the continued existence of Ulster's constitution should be deeply grateful and he is certainly one to whom history will be kind'.[13]

The matters which concerned Chichester-Clark most were the swift elimination of 'no-go' areas and the strength of feeling amongst many of the less well-off communities. Had he experienced a mixture of better luck, greater support and less obscurantism, then he would have had more success in his unenviable role as Prime Minister of Northern Ireland. As it was, without enthusiastic encouragement and vigorous support, he was, quite unjustifiably, consigned to the role of just another of Ulster's fallen premiers.

---

[13] *Unionist,* April 1971

13

The Years Roll On

The King is dead, long live the King. The day after Chichester-Clark's resignation, the eyes of the world were focussed on who would succeed him as Prime Minister of Northern Ireland. The past efforts and struggles of the outgoing premier were forgotten and laid aside. To James Chichester-Clark this was exactly as it was supposed to be. He now had time to get on with his own life. He was not the kind of person to be hankering after lost power. It was for someone else to try to succeed in the great endeavour of bringing peace to the Province. He wished that person well – whoever it might be. And, for a moment, he thought of the significant events which had occurred in the world throughout his time in office. In the United Kingdom, the QE2 had undertaken her maiden voyage, Concorde flew for the first time and, just a few weeks before his resignation, Britain had 'gone decimal'. In other parts of the world, the Biafran War was raging, Charles de Gaulle had died, Tony Jacklin had won the US Open golf championship and, most spectacularly of all, men had walked on the surface of the moon in July 1969. In context, therefore, the tragedy of Northern Ireland faded into insignificance for the observers of world affairs, though not, of course, for those suffering in Northern Ireland.

At Stormont on the following Tuesday, 23 March 1971, the Prime Ministerial baton had been passed – at last thought many – to the ever ambitious Brian Faulkner. He had had only one opponent in the race for the post and that was the still acquisitive William Craig. In the end, it was a 'no contest'. Faulkner easily won by 26 votes to 4. Jimmy Faulkner, Brian's equally ambitious father, had lived to see his son become the Prime Minister of Northern Ireland. This had been his major goal in life. It was hard to say who was the more pleased – Brian or Jimmy. But the fact was plain. Brian Faulkner was, at the age of 50, in the top job, 22 years after first taking his seat as the Member of Parliament for South Down in 1949, when his biggest concern at the time had been the proposed closure of the Belfast and County Down railway. But the problems of 1949 were of no consequence to those he faced in March 1971. His time in office was to prove to be even more turbulent than that of his predecessor, James Chichester-Clark.

At Stormont on Thursday 18 March, Chichester-Clark's last words as Prime Minister concerned his visit to Downing Street a day or so previously. 'Whether or not my visit to London was worthwhile can and will be judged in the next few days by what those troops, and those already here, do'.[1] At that time he did not know that these words were to be his last for he did not think that he would be making up his mind to resign so quickly. But, after the abortive and completely unnecessary visit of Lord Carrington on Saturday morning 20 March and to the complete surprise of Edward Heath in London and most in Northern Ireland, he made up his mind at Moyola Park that Saturday evening. His decision was final and irrevocable. He had made his very best efforts which had been unappreciated by so many, yet valued by a clear majority. In the end he was relieved that he had made his choice to resign after those 689 days as Prime Minister of Northern Ireland.

In the early afternoon at Stormont on Tuesday 23 March, MPs were debating relevant parliamentary matters. The atmosphere was somewhat surreal in that there was no leader in their midst; there was no Prime Minister. The former was absent, somewhere at home looking after his farm. 'One is reminded of one of those rugged ancient heroes who was called from his farm to save the state and, having done so, returned to his farm'.[2] His absence was, of course, only to be expected. Former premiers do not return to the chamber until a decent time has elapsed. Meanwhile, as Opposition members were behaving almost like school children whose teacher was out of the room, taunting those on the government benches, the former Minister of Home Affairs, Robert Porter, was paying tribute to the member for South Londonderry. The member for Belfast Dock, Mr Gerry Fitt, had been in full flow early in the debate and was being rebuffed by Porter for his lack of courtesy in not firstly making mention of the former premier. 'I must confess to feeling a great deal of disappointment

---

[1] *Hansard col 712*, 18 March 1971

[2] *Unionist*, April 1971

that the hon. Member for Dock (Mr Fitt) had not the bigness of mind and spirit to make the slightest acknowledgement of my right hon. and gallant Friend the Member for South Londonderry (Major Chichester-Clark) for the services he has rendered without stint and without regard to his own position during the past very difficult months in particular'.[3] Suitably chastened, the ever affable Gerry Fitt was pleased to offer his words of thanks to a Prime Minister whom he said had always done his best in trying circumstances. At 4.15 p.m., however, the House was put out of its suspense. The new Prime Minister, Mr Faulkner, entered the chamber to cheers. His first words at the Dispatch Box sounded clear and fulsome. 'I think that the best tribute I can pay to my right hon. and gallant Friend is to say that at all times he behaved like an officer and a gentleman'.[4] The formalities over, the House got down to the business of finding solutions to dilemmas which had, to date, proved elusive. The succeeding months were to bring yet more terror and sorrow to an already suffering people. The years of the Troubles had taken firm root.

During the final twelve months of the existence of the Northern Ireland Parliament, James Chichester-Clark took little further interest in the happenings in a House he had regularly attended from 1960, when he had first been elected as MP for South Londonderry. He considered that it would be wise not to interfere with the performance of his successor as his predecessor, Terence O'Neill, had done with him from time to time. What the constituents thought of not having their member attending parliament to fight for their own interests is not known, although Chichester-Clark continued to deal diligently with his constituency matters. He put in just three further appearances. On 27 May 1971 he voted for the government on the Finance Bill. He travelled again to Stormont on 13 October 1971 when he supported Faulkner's government against a censure motion brought against it by William Craig. He voted in the division for Faulkner. He returned to Stormont on 25 January 1972 for his final appearance, again to give support to Faulkner in yet another censure debate tabled by the ever troublesome Craig on traditional parades. Chichester-Clark left that day, his last in Stormont. He did not contribute to the debates on any of these occasions. And so, for the final time, the name of 'Moyola, Major the right hon. Baron' appeared in Northern Ireland Hansard.

---

[3] *Hansard col 750*, 23 March 1971

[4] *Ibid. col 760*

Above: James Chichester-Clark meets Prime Minister, Edward Heath, and Home Secretary, Reginald Maudling, at 10 Downing Street, 1970 (*The Times*)

Below: James, Lord Moyola, and his wife Moyra, Lady Moyola, stand on the lawns of Moyola Park, January 2000 (*Clive Scoular*)

Above: James Chichester-Clark, with his daughter, Tara, at her wedding at the Crypt Chapel at the House of Lords, June 1984 (*Family collection*)

Below: On the day of his introduction to the House of Lords as Baron Moyola of Castledawson, accompanied by his sponsors, the Earl of Donegall (left) and Lord Templemore (right), 8 December 1971 (*The Press Association, London*)

The present Moyola Park House, built in 1768, with the less ambitious extension on the right hand side constructed in the late 1920s (*Clive Scoular*)

Left: The 18th century Georgian mansion 'Gravesend' which serves as Moyola Park Golf Clubhouse (*Clive Scoular*)

Right: Castledawson Parish Church, situated at the main gates to the Moyola Park estate and in which graveyard are buried the Dawson family ancestors (*Clive Scoular*)

Left: The difficult, and beautifully situated, 17th green at Moyola Park Golf Club with the falls on the river Moyola in the background (*Clive Scoular*)

However, along with two other former Ministers, Sir Robert Porter and Dr Robert Simpson, he made a controversial statement in the press concerning the short-sightedness and intransigence of the Ulster Unionist '66 Committee' of backbenchers over their opposition to any future political initiatives of the British government. 'We consider it is the duty of us all to study any possible initiative which may lead to the restoration of peace in Northern Ireland. For that reason, we can only regard it as irresponsible of public representatives to take up prepared positions before it is even known what initiatives are, in fact, to be proposed'.[5] This outburst from Lord Moyola was widely seen as an unfortunate intrusion as it was coming from a man who had not been in recent and regular touch with the thinking of his parliamentary colleagues. The sentiments may well have been worthy but they were seen as irrelevant and went down like a 'lead balloon'. His comments not only enraged his fellow MPs, but they clearly jeopardised his position as MP for South Londonderry. It caused a storm and one of his constituency representatives declared that 'it had rendered the former Prime Minister's seat untenable in the eyes of the unionist voters of South Derry. The only course open to him now was to resign'.[6]

On 31 October 1972, Lord Moyola announced that he would not be seeking re-election as MP for South Londonderry. He had had enough of the difficult and angry constituency meetings which he no longer enjoyed. He did not wish any recurrence of the occasion at Maghera when his car was almost overturned by an angry crowd of his own so-called supporters. He could not face a further round of votes of 'no confidence' in him. It was time to go and, wanting to spike the guns of his troublesome constituency association members, he announced his intention not to seek re-election for any new parliament or assembly which might be set up in Northern Ireland. 'I feel it is only right and proper that I should make plain that I do not intend to seek re-election again'.[7] The news was greeted with much pleasure by many of the South Londonderry constituency members, but undoubtedly with dismay and resignation by many of the more moderate members of that association.

It looked as if the long line of Chichesters, Clarks and Chichester-Clarks as Members of Parliament for South Londonderry had come to an end. Fifty years had now elapsed since the opening of the Northern Ireland

---

[5] *Irish Times*, 16 March 1972

[6] *Ibid.*

[7] *Ibid.*, 31 October 1972

Parliament in 1921 and since then South Londonderry's MPs had all three been members of their family – Mrs Dehra Chichester (later to become Dame Dehra Parker), from 1921 until 1929 and then from 1933 until 1960; Captain J. J. L-C. Chichester-Clark, from 1929 until his untimely death in 1933, and lastly, James D. Chichester-Clark, from 1960 until 1972. Even had Stormont not been prorogued in March 1972, it never seemed likely that either of James Chichester-Clark's two daughters or his stepson would have had the wish or inclination to seek nomination for the seat.

Ennoblement

On Saturday 12 June 1971, the Belfast morning newspapers carried the bold headline, 'Life Peerage for Chichester-Clark'. The new Baron Moyola of Castledawson was the sole Ulsterman to have been elevated to the peerage in the Queen's Official Birthday honours list. It had scarcely been three months since his resignation but the honour for the former Prime Minister was widely welcomed. In truth, it had probably been expected. The local press was obviously pleased as it described the new life peer as one who had 'throughout his Premiership...stuck rigidly to the promised line of seeing reforms through'.[8] The family at home was satisfied with what seemed a well deserved honour, but the new Lord Moyola was characteristically modest about the whole affair. He had also become the first of the long line of Chichesters and their successors to have been so honoured – the first Moyola Park peer of the realm to sit in the House of Lords. He took, as his title, Baron Moyola of Castledawson and prominent on his new coat of arms, under the motto 'Virtute et Labore' (through honesty and labour or by strength and hard work), were emblazoned three red swords charged with a shamrock green. This was a fitting heraldic crest and affirmation for the new Lord Moyola. It was on 8 December 1971 that he travelled to London to be introduced into the House of Lords, the Upper House of parliament. His supporters for the ceremony of introduction to the House, when he took the oath and was sworn in, were the Earl of Donegall and Lord Templemore. Both these men were relatives of the new Baron. After briefly taking his seat on the Conservative benches, Lord Moyola retired to the outer reaches of the House to be interviewed by waiting journalists. A former Prime Minister of Northern Ireland continued

---

[8] *News Letter*, 12 June 1971

to be a centre of attraction for the press barons of Fleet Street and of the provincial newspapers of his homeland.

Baron Moyola made his maiden speech in the Lords during 1973. In truth he found his noble colleagues very open and friendly and he soon made many contacts. He attended the House on as many occasions as he felt able to travel there from Northern Ireland and made a number of contributions to the debates, particularly on matters affecting the Province and on agriculture. However, he soon found the travelling to their Lordships' House too difficult and time-consuming and consequently sought, and was granted, a 'leave of absence'. After 1980, he rarely graced the chamber of the House, although he did speak in the acrimonious debates which followed the signing of the Anglo-Irish Agreement on 15 November 1985. In a feisty speech, in which he denigrated many of the government Ministers for their 'treachery', he expressed his own opposition, and that of so many others, to the agreement. His speech drew much praise from friend and foe alike. It was his finest hour in that place.

The demise of the Northern Ireland Parliament

On his resignation, Chichester-Clark could only imagine the troubles which would affect Brian Faulkner during his tragically short reign as Prime Minister. He turned his attention from Stormont to the day to day responsibilities of running his farm. His family was pleased to see him at home again. It seemed a long time since husband and father was sure to be around for meals at regular times. Politics now took a very low profile although he was very conscious of the deterioration in the fabric of Northern Ireland society. He understood, of course, what terrors were facing his successor. He had, after all, experienced them himself. He was not envious of Faulkner's difficult task. He did not, however, realise how quickly the institutions of the state would disintegrate as happened with such alarming rapidity. Before Faulkner's tempestuous year was out, a catalogue of infamy was visited upon the Province.

In the summer, the new Prime Minister bowed to pressure from within and introduced internment. A better informed and properly organised series of arrests might have proved almost acceptable, but the fact that those interned in August 1971 were all Catholics and were only the young and old, and certainly not any active insurrectionists, turned public opinion totally against the increasingly beleaguered Faulkner. The step had been an unmitigated disaster, a view agreed by almost everyone. Lord Moyola, who had had a brief experience of short term internment and who was one of those who thought that Faulkner's move had been calamitous, felt that if the Prime Minister had needed to introduce such a fateful step, then it would have been far better just to intern a relatively small number, perhaps fifty. He considered that Faulkner had spent too much time contemplating the move and, of course, when he made it, things had all turned against him.

Deaths and killings escalated, subjecting the people of Belfast and other towns and cities to an unspeakable horror. The slaughter following the explosion at McGurk's bar which resulted in 15 deaths and untold numbers of dreadful injuries, was only overshadowed by the events of Bloody Sunday in Londonderry on 30 January 1972. The world was appalled at what it had seen on the television screens. There seemed little future for the unionist administration of Faulkner and, at the end of March, Edward Heath took the final and fateful step of proroguing the Stormont Parliament. After just over 50 years the hegemony of Ulster Unionist power abruptly came to an end. To Faulkner and his Cabinet there seemed little to live for, with nothing but political oblivion in prospect. Lord Moyola had his own view. 'I would have fought tooth and nail against it'.[9] He was horrified that Stormont had been prorogued and observed that, as the British government really knew precious little about the Province, Faulkner and his Cabinet should have refused to go. But he failed to remember that a Province with a Prime Minister with no control over security was like having a car without an engine. Lord Moyola eventually admitted that his view for a continuance of Northern Ireland, as he had known it, was totally unrealistic. A Secretary of State, William Whitelaw, arrived to face the population, which wondered what the changes would bring. Many were pleased that the hated unionist regime was no more, but the feeling of the majority was simply one of uncertainty. Whitelaw proved to be a kind and gentle man who did make mistakes but who was largely forgiven for his genuine faux pas. Unfortunately he could not stop the carnage perpetrated upon the ordinary civilians, Catholic and Protestant. In that first year of direct rule 467 were killed, including a staggering 95 in the month of July, a horrific number swollen by the events of Bloody Friday and the Oxford Street bus station bomb.

---

[9] *Belfast Telegraph*, 25 February 1993

Whitelaw's attempts at bringing the political parties together had some degree of initial success. In September 1972, he chaired talks in Darlington with some of the Northern Ireland parties including Faulkner's Ulster Unionists. Although these discussions did not achieve a great deal, his tenacity paid off by the end of 1973 when the Sunningdale Conference paved the way for the first ever power sharing Executive in the history of Northern Ireland. Elections had brought together 78 members of all political hues and, although Paisley's Democratic Unionist Party inevitably refused to participate, an Executive, consisting of Ulster Unionist, SDLP and Alliance politicians, met for the first time on 1 January 1974. However, the pressures on Faulkner were extraordinarily difficult. No sooner had he taken his seat at Stormont than he was defeated in a vote of confidence by the members of the Ulster Unionist Council on 4 January. He now felt that he had no alternative but to sever his links with a party he had joined nearly 30 years previously. With astonishing speed, Faulkner's old adversary (and that, too, of Lord Moyola), Harry West, became leader of the Ulster Unionist Party.

The Executive, as is well known, did not last long. Although the new Ministers went about their tasks with great gusto, their efforts were to no avail. In May, a previously unknown grouping, the Ulster Workers' Council, brought the Province to its knees by means of a strike which struck terror into the hearts of every citizen. In less than two weeks, and with the impotent Labour government taking no effective action to break the strike, the bully boys had achieved a remarkable success. Without power, electricity, fresh food and fuel, the Province did not survive and, on 27 May, Faulkner and his Executive resigned. The experiment in sharing power had collapsed in the face of a firm and resolute Protestant minority which showed that brute force still proved to be the only effective method in bringing down their hated Executive. During the strike, Lord Moyola and his family had fared reasonably well since they had their own electricity supply which they shared with as many of their neighbours as they could. Like others who were in a position to do so, he laid low and awaited the outcome of this humiliating episode in Northern Ireland's history. As a firm supporter of power sharing, Lord Moyola felt that a wonderful opportunity had once again been missed. His prophesy in an interview with Barry White of the *Belfast Telegraph* on 25 February 1993, almost twenty years after the event, shows the high calibre of Lord Moyola. 'If that day (when violence stops) comes – and he remains an optimist – he is absolutely certain that there will be talks with Sinn Fein. But not before'.[10] Now, at the beginning of this new millennium and with the brokering of the Good Friday Agreement, we can only but be impressed by Lord Moyola's foresight.

In the political chaos which ensued, Brian Faulkner determined to carry on in politics. He founded the Unionist Party of Northern Ireland (UPNI) which was officially launched in September 1974. Many moderate unionists rallied to the cause, including James Moyola, in the hope that they might be able to break the stranglehold of the more extreme unionist elements. Although he had been non-committal about breaking with the Unionist party earlier, especially when he had blasted William Craig, in November 1972, about Craig's Vanguard Unionist Party talking seriously about a Unilateral Declaration of Independence (UDI), he did not break his links at that time. The new party met with little success. It contested a number of local, national and European elections over the next seven years, but failed to make any impression on the electorate. Their appeal for moderation fell, if not on totally deaf ears, then certainly on those whose hearing was dim. By 1976, Faulkner could see no future in politics and resigned the leadership of the UPNI, passing the baton to the first ever woman leader of a Northern Ireland political party, Anne Dickson. Lord Moyola tried his best in the House of Lords to keep the voice of unionist moderation alive in that hallowed chamber and acted as a UPNI spokesman for a number of years. He was assisted in his endeavours in the Upper House by John Brooke, who had succeeded to the Brookeborough Viscountcy on the death of his father in 1973. In 1981, long after the tragic death of its founder, Brian (Lord) Faulkner, and with no prospects of a brighter electoral future, Mrs Dickson and her UPNI executive wound up the Party. With no official Northern Ireland party tag any longer, James Moyola reverted to his Conservative whip in the Lords. To have been part of a long line of loyal supporters of unionist politics in Northern Ireland since its inception in 1921, it came as a great blow to him to suddenly find himself without any Ulster affiliation. It now seemed rather anonymous to be a mere Tory camp follower. He looked back at the damage that Northern Ireland had inflicted on itself and ruefully admitted that the British government could not be blamed for everything.

---

[10] *Belfast Telegraph,* 25 February 1993

Terror stalks the land

As year succeeded year, so terror was piled on terror. As the seventies progressed, so also did the slaughter of innocent civilians, the destruction of property and the cynical and cold blooded murder of members of the security forces. The terrorists, too, suffered their own deprivations. The headlines of the newspapers, day by day and month on month, catalogued the grim statistics of the systematic annihilation of Northern Ireland. The emergence of the Protestant terror gangs brought abject fear to the Catholic community. The alienation of formerly good Catholic and Protestant neighbours continued. The wickedness of the fire bombing of the La Mon House Hotel and the vicious murder of Lord Mountbatten and the eighteen soldiers that very same day numbed a society whose capacity to withstand such horrors had almost been stretched beyond its limit. There were, of course, occasional flickers of hope such as the outflow of support for the Peace People (itself born out of tragedy) but it, like many other attempts at reconciliation, foundered in the face of obscurantism and obfuscation from those whose sole goal it was to bring pain and suffering, not peace and harmony.

A golf course for Moyola Park

An early venture for Lord Moyola in the first years following his retirement from politics was to decide to build an eighteen hole golf course on the Moyola Park estate. Although Lady Moyola's mother had, in her youth, been an Ulster golf champion, golf was not in the blood of Lord and Lady Moyola. They were not ardent golfers. With a real desire to be rid of the vagaries of the European Common Agricultural Policy and with an eye to taking life a bit easier, the decision was made to drastically reduce their farm animal numbers and to change from farming to leisure. This was, therefore, a purely hard headed business decision, for the Moyolas knew that golf was Ireland's favourite sport and the early 1970s was the time to expand facilities for the ever growing number of golf enthusiasts throughout the island. Castledawson was an ideal location which would certainly benefit from having a golf course. Construction began in 1975, with much of the labour being undertaken by the members of the family. Lord Moyola himself recalls the pleasure he experienced in the hard physical work connected with building the golf course under the expert tutelage of Mr Don Patterson and the watchful eye of landscape architect, Mr Alan Smith. Cutting trees, reshaping ditches and digging out bunkers seemed the ideal antidote to dealing with the capriciousness of Ulster politicians. And, to his chagrin, he also remembers that one of his hardest workers on the course was Thomas McElwee who, later in his life, was to become one of the hunger strikers who died at the Maze Prison. His death occurred on 8 August 1981, after 65 days. He was one of the ten men who refused to call off their campaign and were martyrs to their cause.

Lord Moyola's maternal great grandfather, Lord Spencer Chichester, had struck the first golf ball on the estate grounds in the very early years of the twentieth century following his return from a holiday in Scotland. He was so taken with the game that he set about making a few makeshift holes on his estate. But these arrangements were solely for his own enjoyment. Over seventy years later, then, it came about that his great-grandson resurrected his ancestor's idea and set about realising the potential of a regulation course within the environs of the Park. Having completed the first nine holes during 1976, work continued apace and saw the completion of the entire eighteen holes by the early part of 1977. There could hardly have been a more perfect location for a golf course. Set, as it is, within such beautiful parkland bordered by the lovely Moyola river, the course, which has a par of 71, has variously been described by golf enthusiasts as a 'dream' and 'one of Ireland's premier golfing experiences'. Jack Magowan, then the golfing correspondent for the *Belfast Telegraph*, sang its praises in his description of one of the holes, 'the 351 yard eighth there is being ranked among the most picturesque and arresting holes in Ulster golf'.[11] It was officially opened by Mr Don Moncrieff on 9 September 1977 and the assembled crowds that day were treated to a fine match involving four of Ireland's greatest players of the day – Christy O'Connor snr., Paul Leonard, Barry Brennan and Norman Drew. Two years later, on 9 August 1979, the club hosted its first pro-am competition which attracted over fifty of Ireland's finest players. Such is the difficulty of the 6519 yard course that not one of the professionals playing that day was able to beat, or even equal, the par of 71. For the record, the winner was Shandon Park, Belfast's professional, Philip Posnett, with a one over par 72. However the most memorable day at Moyola Park Golf Club was surely 11 August 1980 when the world renowned Spanish golfer, Severiano Ballesteros, came to give a golf clinic and play in an exhibition match with Irish players Des

---

[11] *Belfast Telegraph*, 9 August 1979

Smyth, Peter McEvoy and David Young. This certainly was a day to remember for golf at Moyola Park with the newspaper headlines hailing 'The Day Sevvy came to Castledawson'.[12] But Lord Moyola recalls the down side of the event – the enormity of the fee for the visitor (reputed to be over £8,000, an exorbitant sum in those days) and the lack of courtesy shown by the player, which left much to be desired. He seemed impatient to get away to his next engagement having been late in arriving.

The clubhouse at Moyola Park Golf Club is a spectacular Georgian house with a fascinating history. This striking mansion, known as 'Gravesend', is almost 300 years old. It was the retirement home of Admiral Lord Graves who had fought, with some distinction, in the battle of the glorious first of June against the French in 1794 during the Napoleonic Wars. The house was bought in 1956 by Lord Moyola along with 56 acres of land. However, when the golf course was built around it, it seemed an ideal choice as the clubhouse. The house was subsequently bought by the golf club from Lord Moyola in 1980, although he continues to own the course itself. All in all the golf course project has been an outstanding success with James Moyola the driving force behind it. It had given both him and his family a great deal of enjoyment and a real sense of achievement. Above all, golfers from near and far came, and continue to come, to take on the challenge of one of Northern Ireland's most appealing and yet most formidable courses.

The tragic death of Brian Faulkner

When James Moyola and his wife heard the news on 3 March 1977, they could not believe their ears. Brian Faulkner, only recently ennobled as Baron Faulkner of Downpatrick and even more recently introduced to the House of Lords, had tragically fallen from his horse during a hunt and had hit his head on the road with such force that the blow had killed him. The man who had succeeded Lord Moyola as Prime Minister in March 1971, and who had been to hell and back in the succeeding years, had just recently retired from politics to enable him to spend more time with his wife and family. His chief delight in life had always been hunting to hounds and, in whatever spare time he had had during the years, he was regularly to be seen astride his favourite mount. The Province was stunned

---

[12] *Belfast Telegraph*, 12 August 1980

at the devastating news and tributes came flowing in from those who had been his political friends and foes. James Moyola added his words of appreciation and condolence. After a private burial service at his home church, Magherahamlet Presbyterian, outside Ballynahinch in County Down, there was a well attended memorial service at Stormont Presbyterian Church, close to Parliament Buildings, on Friday 11 March 1977. The country had lost a worthy, professional and hard-working politician, a fact evidenced by the large congregation that day which included people from all walks of life in Northern Ireland and from further afield. Thus the agony for Northern Ireland continued.

Recognition from London

On 8 June 1978, a bulletin from the Honourable The Irish Society proclaimed the good news that James Moyola had been made a Freeman of the City of London. It will be remembered that most of County Londonderry had been 'planted' in previous centuries by the London Companies and they continued to show an interest in this part of Northern Ireland by bestowing, at regular intervals, freedoms on prominent local dignitaries. The announcement declared that 'Lord Moyola is delighted to have been made a Freeman of the most famous metropolis in the world'[13] and, in a quirky riposte, he himself said how pleased he was, although he had discovered that there did not even come a free parking space with the honour. However, in a more serious vein, the secretary of the Irish Society did say that 'Lord Moyola is one of several heads of the community across the political divide we are honouring in the Coleraine and Londonderry area for good works they have carried out'.[14] The ceremony was a glittering affair attended by all the latest recipients and Lord Moyola was particularly pleased that a similar honour had been bestowed upon his good friend, and constituency ally, Mr George McIlrath. It was good to realise that he had not been forgotten and that his continuing good works were being recognised in such a tangible way.

---

[13] *Belfast Telegraph,* 8 June 1978

[14] *Ibid.*

The years stretch into the eighties

Life in Northern Ireland at the start of the eighties, rather than getting better, was becoming more and more stressful. At the Maze Prison, outside Belfast, a number of republican inmates commenced a hunger strike for five demands from the government, including the right to wear their own clothing and not to participate in prison work. They had, however, reckoned without Margaret Thatcher. They ought to have remembered that 'the lady was not for turning'. And so it proved with her determination not to give in to the demands of these men. Try as they could to force a change of heart, the British Prime Minister did not relent, thus allowing for only one outcome – the death of one or more of the hunger strikers. However, before the strike had entered its most critical stage, one of their number and the leader of the prison protest, Bobby Sands, was nominated to stand for the Westminster by-election in Fermanagh/South Tyrone which had been caused by the death of the Independent MP, Frank Maguire. Sands campaigned from his prison cell and, in an extraordinary show of nationalist unity (and in the face of opposition from SDLP supporters for their party's decision not to contest the seat) Sands won the seat by a majority of 1,446 votes over the Ulster Unionist, Harry West. He only held the seat from 9 April until his death, on the sixty-sixth day of his hunger strike, on 5 May 1981. The victory, however – followed as it was by the subsequent by-election when Sands' election agent, Owen Carron, held the seat with an increased majority – produced world-wide interest in the republican cause in Northern Ireland and did much to dent Margaret Thatcher's case abroad. Support for her at home in Great Britain was, nonetheless, as strong as ever. Before the strike eventually ended at the beginning of October, ten men had died, but sadly over sixty people had been killed, including thirty members of the security forces, in a continuing escalation of violence in the Province.

During this time, Lord Moyola could only sit and reflect on the deterioration of law and order. One of the hunger strikers had worked on his golf course project before being convicted and jailed for terrorist activities in the Ballymena area. This man had been well liked by Lord Moyola and by the others working on the project. Lord Moyola gave unequivocal support to the government's stance during the entire hunger strike saga. He and his family were horrified at the continuing wave of death and destruction but were powerless to do anything about it.

Earlier in the year, Lord Moyola had spoken out in the press about the continued irresponsible attitude of Ian Paisley and his cohorts. Over the years, he had become increasingly enraged at the DUP leader's diatribes. He was widely quoted in his condemnation of the Protestant demagogue. 'Paisley's recent activities could jeopardise the province's future'.[15] Lord Moyola further warned of the lasting detrimental effect of Paisley's outpourings on British public opinion. 'Lord Moyola has taken the opportunity to remind Ulster men and women of the danger of antagonising our friends in the UK by some Ulster loyalists adopting attitudes and proclaiming threats which he does not feel are justified at this stage'.[16] What Lord Moyola was saying was plain for all sensible people to see. Public opinion in Great Britain to the antics of some of the more vociferous elements in Northern Ireland was certainly having a negative and devastating effect on their attitude to the continuing union between Great Britain and the Province. It bode ill for the majority in Northern Ireland to be associating with Paisley's remarks for there were many in Great Britain who felt that the time had come to set Northern Ireland adrift. But Lord Moyola's words fell on deaf ears. Paisley simply passed over the remarks of the former Prime Minister as he would have squished a fly on the lapel of his overcoat.

The Falklands War and continuing crises in the Province

Life became increasingly difficult for the citizens of Northern Ireland. Horrendous occurrences such as the brutal assassination of the Ulster Unionist MP, the Reverend Robert Bradford in November 1981 and the deaths in the Droppin' Well public house in Ballykelly close to Christmas 1982 only proved, if such evidence was necessary, that the cruel determination of the IRA to sever the link with the United Kingdom showed no sign of ending.

For a moment at least, the outbreak of the Falklands War in April 1982 took the spotlight off the troubles in Northern Ireland. Margaret Thatcher again displayed her utter will and resolution in seeing off the aggression of the Argentine dictator, General Galtieri, upon the defenceless people of the Falkland Islands. Lord Moyola was full of admiration for the

---

[15] *News Letter,* 11 February 1981

[16] *Ibid.*

156

British Prime Minister's unequivocal action in sending the Task Force to expel the Argentines with such a show of ruthless and speedy determination.

That same year, 1982, the Secretary of State, Jim Prior, continued with his political initiatives despite much opposition and intransigence from the local politicians. Assembly elections were held in October 1982 but there was the usual in-fighting amongst the parties resulting in another round of boycotting by some of the Assembly groupings. Lord Moyola, at home in Castledawson, could only stand and stare. He remained despondent about the future for the Province which he had led some ten years previously. After so many attempts to move forward, there seemed to be very few signs of political maturity. Nothing, he reflected, had changed.

Disappointment in the High Court

In June 1983, Lord Moyola went to the High Court with a view to trying to save his family from crippling taxes after his death. He petitioned to change his marriage settlement (which had been drawn up a few days before his wedding in March 1959) to make the two daughters of his marriage, Fiona and Tara, the sole beneficiaries to the family fortunes and to make Fiona the heir to Moyola Park. In a complicated judgement, however, Lord Justice Murray ruled against Lord Moyola on the grounds that he could not change his marriage settlement which mentioned the 'children of the marriage' as there could yet be subsequent children. The judgement greatly disappointed the Moyolas and, to add insult to injury, the costs of the case were awarded against them.

A wedding in the family

On 15 June 1984, the Moyolas' second daughter, Tara, was married to Edward Whitley. Tara, then just 21 years old, had met her husband in London. The ceremony took place in the Crypt Chapel at the House of Lords and was solemnised by the incumbent Chapel priest. It was a beautifully hot day and perfect for the occasion. As the Chapel only held a relatively small number of people, the guest list was restricted to around 40 family and close friends. The reception took place at the home of the bride's step brother, Michael. The young couple spent their first married years in Hong Kong and then in London. They now live in East Sussex with their son, James.

Lord Moyola speaks up

Later in the year of his daughter's wedding, the IRA bombing of the Grand Hotel in Brighton during the Conservative Party Conference caused outrage and consternation. Five senior Tories had succumbed and it was only good luck which prevented the Prime Minister herself from being killed as well. Lord Moyola, shocked as he was at an event of such horrific effrontery, realised one thing. He knew that Margaret Thatcher would now, finally, put her mind to finding a lasting solution to the problems of Northern Ireland. But the solution appalled and saddened Lord Moyola.

The outcome took the form of the Anglo-Irish Agreement signed at Hillsborough on 15 November 1985. He was critical of the total lack of consultation with the Unionist majority and considered that the agreement was 'a step too far'.[17] However, James Moyola was a pragmatist. Although he felt that Margaret Thatcher had acted unadvisedly, he was realistic enough to know that she would never change her mind. The attitude of Ulster Unionists was perhaps understandable, and their actions, such as their MPs resigning their Westminster seats to fight by-elections, were entirely predictable. But Lord Moyola knew that sooner or later discussions would have to take place. Not even intransigent Ulster politicians could remain outside forever. Consequently, in April 1986, along with Viscount Brookeborough, he bearded Margaret Thatcher in her 10 Downing Street den. Although he had met the 'Iron Lady' once before, when he had found her to be most agreeable and helpful, this time he found her in a different frame of mind. Brookeborough and he were subjected to a diatribe on what should and should not be done in Northern Ireland. The meeting was not a success and the Ulster peers left Downing Street with their tails between their legs. They had tried to explain their more moderate views – but to little avail. As Lord Moyola reflected on the events of those past months, he could only suggest, to those who cared to listen, that it had been a bad day's work when the link between the Tories in London and the Ulster Unionists in Belfast had been broken. 'He thinks that if the Unionists had

---

[17] *Belfast Telegraph*, 25 February 1993

been aligned with the Conservatives, the Anglo-Irish Agreement might not have been signed'.[18] He also lambasted the alliance between the Official Ulster Unionists and the Democratic Unionist Party as never the way to win friends and influence people. And, by way of yet another prophesy from one whom many considered to be out of touch with current political thought, James Moyola declared that if the Republic of Ireland had dropped Articles Two and Three of their constitution back in 1985, then the outcome for those in Northern Ireland would have been better. It took a further fourteen years for those Articles to be finally expunged in December 1999 at the time of the final peace deal, following the 1998 Good Friday Agreement. Let no one say, therefore, that Lord Moyola's political sensibilities have been dulled. His prognostications of 1985 and 1986 have come to be realised.

However Lord Moyola remained sceptical about the benefits, or otherwise, of the Anglo-Irish Agreement and in June 1986, after his abortive attempt to influence Margaret Thatcher the previous April, he became a trustee of the newly formed Friends of the Union. This was an organisation set up to 'increase knowledge and understanding of the need to maintain the union of Great Britain and Northern Ireland' and its trustees and patrons (one of whom was Robin Chichester-Clark) were mostly opposed to the Anglo-Irish Agreement. They continued to lobby the Prime Minister but with very little success. The organisation fairly soon became inactive and ineffectual and faded from the scene as quickly as it had appeared.

As the years went by, even Margaret Thatcher could feel the almost tangible sense of outrage of the people in the Province. She visited from time to time and met politicians from every quarter on each occasion. When the IRA exploded their bomb during the Armistice Day ceremony in Enniskillen in November 1987, the stark reality of the fears of most sane and sensible people in Northern Ireland were brought home to her. She was a chastened lady as she joined with the bereaved at a memorial service in Enniskillen a few days later. Throughout her remaining years as the chatelaine of 10 Downing Street, she increasingly understood the trials and tribulations of the vast majority of all persuasions in Northern Ireland. In her quieter moments she perhaps realised that she should have listened to James Moyola, and other like minded Ulstermen and women, instead of lecturing to them.

---

[18] *Belfast Telegraph*, 25 February 1993

However, bombings, murder and destruction stalked the highways and byways of Northern Ireland for the years to come. Lord Moyola could only consider at what might have been. He gave occasional interviews for the newspapers over the remaining years of the second millennium. Readers would have said 'Is he still around'? But they would hardly have taken much notice of a man who had been given very little credibility in days gone by. It might have been better for them all to have listened to a man whose foresight and prophesies have come to fruition in these days of early 2000. The seeds sown in reform after reform in 1969 and 1970 have, thirty years later in 1999 and 2000, produced a harvest which will, at long last, bring peace to the people of Northern Ireland, Great Britain and the Republic of Ireland. Perhaps the evils of the past centuries may now be buried once and for all. The words of an editorial in the *Belfast Telegraph* very adequately sum up the position. 'But Lord Moyola can reflect that at least he tried when so many others gave up. That he had to struggle against odds, that he was prepared to face the strains and loneliness of his office, adds honour to the man'.[19] This surely is a fitting tribute to this quiet and determined man of Northern Irish politics.

Lord and Lady Moyola now take pleasure in their vacations abroad. They enjoy seeing their children and grandchildren. They revel in their peaceful home at Moyola Park beside that lovely river Moyola. This is only right for a politician and gentleman whose story has now been told. He must be remembered as a leading player and not as one in a supporting role.

---

[19] *Belfast Telegraph,* 31 October 1972

14

Conclusion

Reliable; sound; decent; straight; determined. A man without guile; approachable and not haughty; one full of integrity. A person who commanded respect; a well organised chairman; one with much foresight. A fine fellow; an honest country gentleman; an easy man with whom to do business. A public duty man; a strong force; a lovely man with whom to work. These words contain the less well known epithets which describe James Chichester-Clark. They are not the adjectives which always flow easily off the tongue – for one reason and for one reason only. This reluctant and unambitious Prime Minister; this premier 'who looked like a reluctant bridegroom arriving at a church';[1] this unwilling head of government has, to date, been written off and passed over in the annals of the state. But a person variously described by all these attributes is much more worthy of a significant place in the well ordered history of Northern Ireland.

Chichester-Clark's invisible interior far outshone his visible exterior. These unseen attributes were far more impressive than many of his visibly unimpressive actions and appearances. He was not a sparkling orator; he freely agreed with the public's perception of his being a very poor television performer; he did not court the image of the trendy gent. Why, then, did this honest and decent man retreat to the hallowed courts of 'Moyola les deux eglises' after a relatively short incumbency at Stormont Castle?

In May 1969 he had seen it as his public duty to come to the rescue of a Province starting to tear itself apart. His decision was mightily unpopular at home. But politics, and the specific brand of Irish politics,

---

[1] *Belfast Telegraph*, 30 April 1970

were in his genes and duty came before self. This was also evidenced by his active service in World War II where the serious injuries he had sustained at Anzio were far more severe than many would ever know.

Terence O'Neill had lost his fervour for power and, being frankly unconvinced that his reforms were getting anywhere, he was finding life becoming a drag. Many of his parliamentary colleagues were losing confidence in him and they knew that this was bad for the Province. O'Neill clearly wanted out and so James Chichester-Clark determinedly took up the baton. It seemed the right thing to do. He was an exemplary successor to the premiership of Northern Ireland, every bit as much as his own successor, Brian Faulkner.

During his period in office, Chichester-Clark experienced as much success as failure. His approach to the task in hand was 'much more subtle than O'Neill's'.[2] He was an open man, prepared to talk to whomsoever wished to speak to him. He never stood on his dignity by requiring appointments to be made and he will be remembered by many ordinary citizens who successfully collared their Prime Minister, either at the end of a meeting in Magherafelt Orange Hall to ask a question about the price of pigs or by bending his ear to the time-worn Ulster method of enquiry – 'can I have a wee word in your ear, Prime Minister'? Terence O'Neill, try as he could, was never able or willing to be so approachable. James Chichester-Clark had a healthy attitude to MPs in the House of Commons. All of them, Opposition members included, had a mandate to be there and deserved his attention. He made time to talk to Gerry Fitt and James O'Reilly just as he endeavoured, not always successfully, to confer with William Craig and Harry West. His openness with his own parliamentary colleagues seemed rarely to be appreciated.

The reforms which he carried through, often against fierce opposition, were effected with speed and alacrity. He must be given credit for the number of the reforms which he was able to put on the statute book. Few, however, have credited him at all, brushing aside his efforts as simply pushing them through at the behest of an ever more persuasive British government. Yet there are many British and international observers who did give Chichester-Clark the credit for the number of reforms he did put through. Being basically a person who made best use of his own resources, Chichester-Clark remained the head of a government which did not have a tendency to panic. Towards the end of his term of office, he should perhaps

---

[2] *Belfast Telegraph,* 30 April 1970

have taken more heed of the advice to make Reginald Maudling listen to him rather than the other way about.

The battles he had to face

In its fifty years in power, the Ulster Unionist Party never had any effective opposition in the Northern Ireland House of Commons. So, particularly in its latter stages, it constructed its own opposition – from within. The party split and split and split again. During Chichester-Clark's incumbency, he constantly had to look over his shoulder and, for a man of his political style, this did not come naturally. Dissident backbenchers, like Boal, McQuade and Warnock, sniped at him and called for more determined action. Politicians, who ought to have known better and who had themselves been numbered amongst the small band of those fit and able to hold the rank of Cabinet Minister, such as Craig and West, ranted and raved, looking for a change of government. Unrealistic and blinkered local politicians – very often in his own South Londonderry constituency – spent nugatory hours in anonymous and remote Orange Halls passing votes of 'no confidence' in their Prime Minister. The deafening roar of the Aughnacloy auctioneers, the Bellaghy butchers and the Castledawson car salesmen demanding satisfaction for their minor complaints, whilst the Province suffered, was heard far and near. And then, to add insult to injury, Ian Paisley and William Beattie won the April 1970 by-elections, thus causing a further erosion in the government ranks. Chichester-Clark, still an optimist at heart, felt more and more dejected.

But possibly the greatest strain on this trusting and respected man was the pressure brought upon him by that unwieldy body, the Ulster Unionist Council. Chichester-Clark certainly found it difficult to face up to these meetings. The world will never know the stresses and strains to which he was regularly subjected within those secretive and mystical surroundings. He did receive standing ovations from the Council but, even then, he could be sure that a large number of the delegates would remain firmly rooted to their seats in an act of petulance and defiance. Votes of 'no confidence' in him as party leader became frequent as the months of his premiership advanced. He had to use every one of his gentlemanly skills to keep his cool. It was never a very happy experience to be so confronted by those who should have been his staunchest allies. In truth, the fact that he no longer had to attend these often fractious meetings after his resignation must have been the greatest relief of all.

As Prime Minister, James Chichester-Clark had many other, more weighty, matters with which to contend. He needed to proceed with his reforms with all speed – and this he did. Within a short space of time he had to face something which no other Prime Minister might have expected; the three contentious reports of the committees which had been set up by the government. Cameron, Hunt and Scarman laid their recommendations before Chichester-Clark in double quick time and, with a British government now realising the errors of its ways and attempting to push Chichester-Clark around, changes occurred with alarming pace. Although most recommendations were perfectly realistic, a number caused no end of additional strife for the already over-burdened premier. The one which created the greatest ruction was the disbandment of the 'B' Specials. Much maligned in nationalist and in certain British circles, the Specials had played their part in the formation of the Province. Chichester-Clark admired them, although he was the first to say that any excesses within the ranks of the Specials ought to be dealt with quickly and without mercy.

Chichester-Clark had also to contend with the arrival of troops in Londonderry following the outbreak of contentious civil strife in the Bogside. The Northern Ireland government, contrary to much critical opinion, had done its best in the ever trying and dangerous circumstances and the Prime Minister had no regrets about calling for troops. They were needed to try to restore order in a troubled city. The attitude of the Taoiseach, Jack Lynch, had been unhelpful, to say the least. Chichester-Clark, although speaking out against him, never held a grudge against the normally gentle Lynch. The emergence of the Provisional IRA passed almost unnoticed at the time, but the ramifications of this IRA split were to change life for ever in Northern Ireland and, for that matter, throughout the island of Ireland.

But it was the 'no-go' areas which tormented Chichester-Clark most of all. They haunted him; they panicked him; they stampeded fear in his mind. In his estimation, these ghettos should have been cleared immediately. Had that happened, then there was every expectation that normality would quickly have been restored to the cities and towns of the Province. But his voice was either not sufficiently well heard or simply ignored. The proliferation of parts of the city where the Queen's writ did not run only served to prolong the agony for the government and the people who lived within these ghettos.

Consequently, despite the undue unhelpfulness of Whitehall, the intransigence of the warring Ulster Unionist Party and the right wing pressures brought upon him by certain of his own parliamentary colleagues, James Chichester-Clark decided that enough was enough. His wife had never been keen on his taking on the role of first citizen and he knew that she would certainly not complain if he resigned. But it was the fact that his own constituents no longer had faith in him that led him to his final decision. They now did not want him as their MP and, as he saw it, if those who had originally elected him were now opposed to what he was doing, it was time to go. He shuddered at the ongoing violence and empathised strongly with those who were suffering and dying. After all, he himself had been himself injured in the horror and chaos of Anzio during World War II. There are many who would ask the question: how can a Prime Minister really understand the suffering of the people? James Chichester-Clark, landed aristocrat and gentleman farmer, was every bit as able to appreciate the sufferings of the population in the Province as any other public figure. The question could also be asked: did the unionist party itself ever know what was happening?

James Chichester-Clark, unambitious and self-effacing as he was, has left an indelible mark on the fabric of Northern Ireland society. He was never the stopgap premier, as many political commentators have portrayed him. He was a man of integrity who worked immensely hard to improve the lot of the people of Northern Ireland. Although he has virtually disappeared from the public view in recent years, he has, on occasion, and even as recently as 1993, prophesied that the engagement of politicians of every hue will lead to a peaceful Province, something which he had not seen since his days as Chief Whip in 1963. The seeds sown by Chichester-Clark in the late sixties are now coming to fruition at the commencement of the third millennium. And he has lived to see this ripening harvest of peace.

Bibliography

Manuscript Materials

Moyola Park , Castledawson

Chichester-Clark Family Papers and Documents

Printed Sources

Parliamentary and other official publications

The Linen Hall Library and its Northern Ireland Political Collection, Belfast

Disturbances in Northern Ireland: report of the Commission (under the Chairmanship of Lord Cameron) [Cmd532], Belfast, 1969. (The Cameron Report)
Report of the Advisory Committee on Police in Northern Ireland [Cmd535], Belfast, 1969. (The Hunt Report)
Violence and Civil Disturbances in Northern Ireland in 1969: report of Tribunal of Inquiry [Cmd566], Belfast, 1972. (The Scarman Tribunal)

Public Record Office of Northern Ireland, Belfast

Northern Ireland House of Commons Debates in Hansard
Northern Ireland Government Cabinet Papers
Ulster Unionist Council Papers

Unpublished PhD Thesis

Mulholland, M., *The Evolution of Ulster Unionism 1960-1969: Causes and Consequences,* The Queen's University of Belfast, 1997.

Secondary Sources

Article

Cochrane, F., *"Meddling at the Crossroads: the Decline and Fall of Terence O'Neill within the Unionist Community"*, in R. English and G. Walker (eds.), *Unionism in Modern Ireland – New Perspectives on Politics and Culture*, Dublin, 1996.

Books

Alexander, Earl, *The Alexander Memoirs*, London, 1962.
Arthur, P. and Jeffrey, K., *Northern Ireland since 1968*, Oxford, 1989.
Bardon, J., *A History of Ulster*, Belfast, 1992.
Bew, P. and Patterson, H., *The British State and the Ulster Crisis*, London, 1985.
Bew, P., Gibbon, P. and Patterson, H., *The State of Northern Ireland 1921-1972*, Manchester, 1979.
Bleakley, D., *Faulkner*, Oxford, 1974.
Bloomfield, K., *Stormont in Crisis – a Memoir*, Belfast, 1994.
Blumenson, M., *Anzio: the Gamble that Failed*, London, 1963.
Bowman, J., *De Valera and the Ulster Question 1917-1973*, Oxford, 1982.
Boyd, A., *Brian Faulkner and the Crisis of Ulster Unionism*, Tralee, 1972.
Callaghan, Rt Hon. J., *A House Divided*, London, 1973.
Card, T., *Eton Renewed – a History from 1860 to the Present Day*, London, 1994.
D'Este, C., *Fatal Decision – Anzio and the Battle for Rome*, London, 1991.
Dwyer, T.R., *De Valera's Finest Hour 1932-1959*, Cork and Dublin, 1982.
Edwards, O.D., *The Sins of our Fathers – Roots of Conflict in Northern Ireland*, Dublin, 1970.
Farrell, M., *Northern Ireland – the Orange State*, London, 1980.
Faulkner, B., *Memoirs of a Statesman*, London, 1978.
Foster, R., *Modern Ireland 1600-1972*, London, 1988.
Gordon, D., *The O'Neill Years*, Belfast, 1989.
Heath, E., *The Autobiography of Edward Heath – The Course of my Life*, London, 1998.
Jackson, A., *Colonel Edward Saunderson: Land and Loyalty in Victorian Ireland*, Oxford, 1995.
Kelly, H., *How Stormont Fell*, Dublin, 1972.
Lee, J.J., *Ireland 1912-1985*, Cambridge, 1989.

Lyons, F.S.L., *Ireland since the Famine*, London, 1973.

MacCurtain, M., *Tudor and Stuart Ireland*, Dublin, 1972.

McIvor, B., *Hope Deferred*, Belfast, 1998.

Moloney, E. and Pollak, A., *Paisley*, Swords, 1986.

Moody, T.W., *The Ulster Question 1603-1973*, Dublin, 1973.

Morgan, K.O., *Callaghan – a Life*, Oxford, 1997.

Neill, Sir I., *A Chorus of Cameos*, Belfast, 1995.

Neill, Sir I., *Church and State*, Belfast, 1995.

Nicolson, N., *Alex, The Life of Field Marshal Earl Alexander of Tunis*, London, 1973.

O'Neill, T.M., *The Autobiography of Terence O'Neill*, London, 1972.

O'Neill, T.M., *Ulster at the Crossroads*, London, 1969.

O'Sullivan, M., *Sean Lemass – a Biography*, Dublin, 1994.

Rose, R., *Governing Without Consensus – an Irish Perspective*, London, 1971.

Sunday Times Insight Team, *Ulster*, Harmondsworth, 1972.

Utley, T.E., *Lessons of Ulster*, London, 1975.

Verney, P., *The Micks – the Story of the Irish Guards*, London, 1970.

Wallace, M., *Northern Ireland – 50 Years of Self Government*, Newton Abbot, 1971.

Wilson, H., *The Labour Government 1964-1970 – a Personal Record*, London, 1971.

Newspapers and Publications

Belfast Central Library, Newspaper Library, Belfast
Northern Ireland Political Collection, The Linen Hall Library, Belfast

Belfast Telegraph
Irish Independent
Irish News
Irish Press
Irish Times
Londonderry Sentinel
Mid Ulster Mail
News Letter
The Daily Mail
The Guardian
The Times
Unionist

Index